Sports Illustrated
FULLthrottle
DAYTONA, DOVER AND BEYOND

Sports Illustrated
FULLthrottle
DAYTONA, DOVER AND BEYOND

BIG RED DALE EARNHARDT JR.,
PHOTOGRAPHED IN RICHMOND, SEPT. 10, 2004.

contents

43'S A CROWD
RICHARD PETTY WAS SURROUNDED BY ADORING FANS AT DAYTONA IN 1975.

PHOTOGRAPH BY JAMES DRAKE

SPORTS ILLUSTRATED

Managing Editor Terry McDonell
President John Squires

Editor Sandra Wright Rosenbush
Art Director Craig Gartner
Senior Editor Richard O'Brien
Photo Editor Jeffrey Weig
Associate Editors Mark Bechtel, Trisha Blackmar, Richard Deitsch
Staff Writers Lars Anderson, Pete McEntegart
Writer-Reporters Mark Beech, Gene Menez, Bill Syken
Reporters Andrew Lawrence, Mark Lelinwalla, Chris Mannix, Craig Mazin
Associate Art Director Karen Meneghin
Assistant Photo Editor Kari Stein
Copy Editors Megan Collins, Rich Donnelly, Denis Johnston, Katherine Pradt, Pamela Ann Roberts
Editorial Assistant Bryan Byers **Administration** Jim Clements
Director, New Product Development Bruce Kaufman

TIME INC. HOME ENTERTAINMENT

President Rob Gursha
Vice President, New Product Development Richard Fraiman
Executive Director, Marketing Services Carol Pittard
Director, Retail & Special Sales Tom Mifsud
Director of Finance Tricia Griffin
Prepress Manager Emily Rabin
Marketing Manager Kristin Rivela
Associate Book Production Manager Suzanne Janso

SPECIAL THANKS:
Bozena Bannett, Alexandra Bliss, Bernadette Corbie, Robert Dente, Anne-Michelle Gallero, Peter Harper, Robert Marasco, Natalie McCrea, Brooke McGuire, Jonathan Polsky, Margarita Quiogue, Mary Jane Rigoroso, Steven Sandonato

COPYRIGHT 2005 TIME INC. HOME ENTERTAINMENT

PUBLISHED BY SPORTS ILLUSTRATED BOOKS

TIME INC.

1271 AVENUE OF THE AMERICAS

NEW YORK, NEW YORK 10020

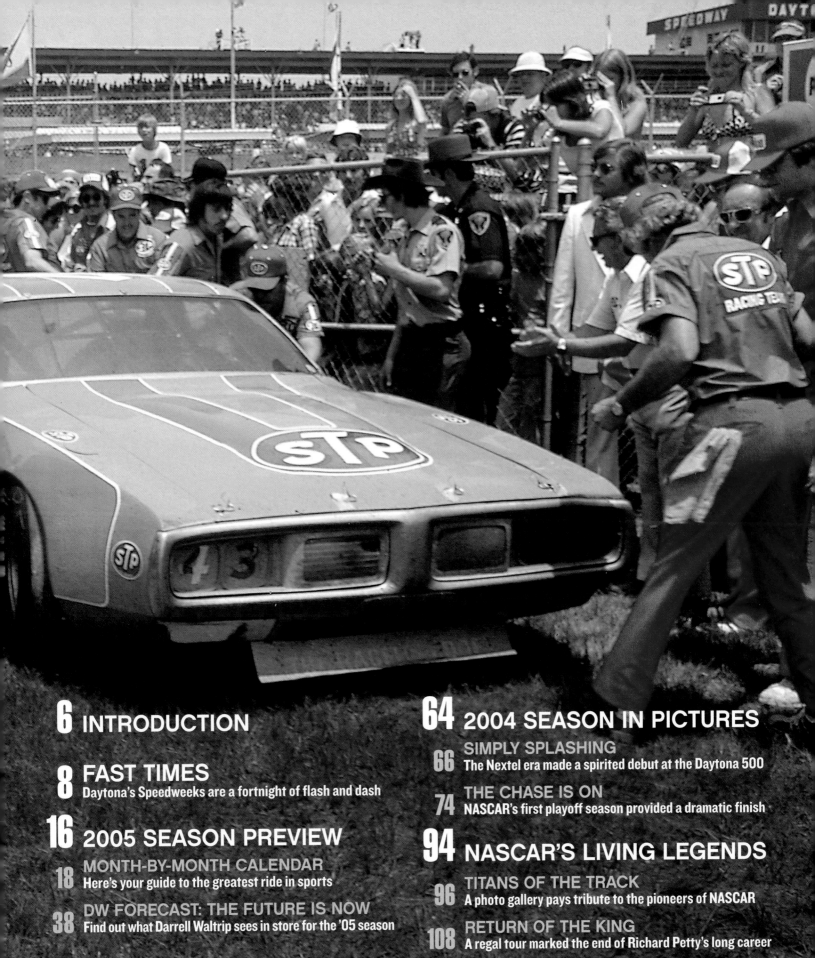

DAVID PEARSON **AGE 70**

introduction
by Richard Deitsch

KURT BUSCH **AGE 26**

ABOVE ALL ELSE, NASCAR IS ABOUT FAMILY.
It's record book is infused with bloodlines—the Pettys, the Earn-hardts, the Allisons, the Jarretts, the Bakers, the Waltrips, the Labontes, the Marlins, the Wallaces. Even the sport's origins and its ongoing leadership are bound by family, beginning with William (Big Bill) France, who begat Bill Jr., who in 2003 passed the baton to Brian, the 42-year-old current chairman and chief executive. Among fans and competitors alike, racing is passed down from generation to generation. Look no further than Nex-tel Cup champion Kurt Busch, who has been mentored by 51-year-old crew chief Jimmy Fennig, who first made a name for himself as a twentysomething crew chief for Bobby Allison, who won Most Popular Driver honors in 1972 when he was piloting a car for Junior Johnson, who sped around dusty North Wilkesboro Speedway in the 1950s before becoming one of the biggest stars in racing.

For a sport anchored by the continuity of family and the (sup-posed) uniformity of its cars, NASCAR underwent some pro-found changes in 2004. First, there was the switch of title sponsor: A tobacco company (Winston) was extinguished for a telecommunications conglomerate (Nextel Communications). Then came a move seen as equally heretical. Last January,

Brian France announced that NASCAR would crown its champion through a 10-race playoff run dubbed the Chase for the Nextel Cup. After the first 26 races of the year, the top 10 dri-vers in the standings (and any others within 400 points of the leader) would have their point totals adjusted so that each was separated from the next by only five points. Then it would be "Start your engines" for a 10-race sprint to the title. While

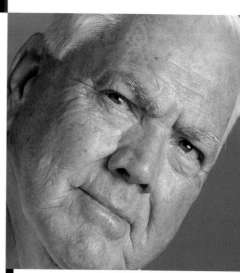

JUNIOR JOHNSON **AGE 73**

many initially regarded the concept as sacrilegious, by the final race at Homestead, converts were everywhere. And why not? The format produced the closest championship finish in the 55 years of NASCAR. "It was probably the single best thing that has happened for race fans in my era," said Mark Martin, who

DALE EARNHARDT JR. AGE 30

JEFF GORDON AGE 33

COTTON OWENS AGE 80

will retire from full-time Cup racing at the end of 2005, after nearly three decades.

Martin, of course, has been around long enough to have tangled with a couple of members of the racing royalty we honor in these pages. In August photographer Greg Foster drove more than 3,500 miles through North and South Carolina to photograph the living legends of NASCAR *(page 94)*, from Johnson to David Pearson to the Allisons to Cale Yarborough. "The competitiveness," Foster says, "is still the common thread among them."

That competitiveness was never more evident than in 2004, when Busch barely held off Jimmie Johnson to win the inaugural Nextel Cup. This season, along with 36 races and 12,518 laps of fender-to-fender competition, we'll see the latest chapter in NASCAR's familial saga: Kyle Busch, who finished second last season in the Busch Series at the tender age of 19, moves up to the Nextel Cup to take over for Terry Labonte in Rick Hendrick's number 5 Chevrolet. "I have a sentimental feeling toward my brother and how I helped him become the driver he is, and how he's helped me," Kurt says. "It's going to be great to race with one another full time—and to hang him out in the draft at Daytona."

What more could any NASCAR brothers want?   □

GREG FOSTER (PEARSON, JUNIOR JOHNSON, OWENS); NIGEL KINRADE (GORDON, EARNHARDT, BUSCH); SAM SHARPE

JIMMIE JOHNSON AGE 29

What better way
to warm the early
days of February
than with a trip
to Daytona for
Speedweeks,
a fortnight of
flash, dash and
fantastic fandom
by Mark Bechtel

fast
TIMES

speedweeks

▲ GORDON SIGNS   ▲ MAYFIELD MINGLES   ▲ WHOOPI STARTS IT UP   ▲ BUSH MEETS BUSCH

IT MAY SEEM A BIT COUNTERINTUITIVE FOR NASCAR TO stage its biggest race of the season first. What could be more dramatic than to hold the Daytona 500 at the end of November, the culmination of nine months of hard racing? What better place to crown the season's champion than at the sport's most-hallowed track? But NASCAR has, for the past 22 years, insisted on opening the season at Daytona, meaning that the 500 is run before any drama has developed—those grudges we love so much have a way of cooling in the off-season. Win the race and what do you get? A big check and a slim lead in the standings that you'll have to try to make hold up for 40 weeks.

And that's just the way it ought to be.

The 500 is preceded by Speedweeks, a fortnight of engine-tuning, wrench-turning and testing. It's a time for fans to meet their heroes—you can't drive around town for five minutes without stumbling upon a driver appearance—and get acquainted with new drivers. It's a rite of spring, one that turns a 2.5-mile tri-oval into a self-sufficient town. Assuming you've got a sizable stash of food (or if you don't mind subsisting on a diet of hot dogs, funnel cakes and turkey legs), there's no reason ever to leave the track.

NASCAR has gone to great lengths to streamline its qualifying process this year, to shorten race weekends. Thankfully, nothing was done to Speedweeks. Daytona 500 qualifying—ironically a rather meaningless event, given that a driver's ability to work the draft is infinitely more important than a good starting spot—is a delightfully drawn-out and arcane process. Days of practice lead to qualifying for two 125-mile races, which in turn set the majority of the field. Then there's the Bud Shootout, a 70-lap non-points race in which many drivers use backup cars, meaning they race with nothing to lose. There's plenty of other racing: ARCA, IROC, Busch and Craftsman Truck series all open their seasons during Speedweeks, whetting the appetites of fans, so that by the time Sunday rolls around, their hunger can only be satisfied by the Great American Race.

We wouldn't have it any other way.

FANFARE

Let the Party Begin

THE DAYTONA 500, NASCAR's most prestigious race, brings out the best in a driver. It also brings out the best in fans, who after suffering through a three-month off-season, pack the grandstands and camp out in the infield throughout Speedweeks. Every year the Daytona 500 draws an estimated 200,000 to the track—many of them out-of-towners who turn the speedway and the surrounding area into one giant beach party. The race attracts big names: In 2004 George W. Bush was in attendance. Naturally the President was a bit conspicuous: Fans not wearing a shirt or hat bearing the name of a driver tend to stick out.

IN THE GARAGE

Tinkering Time

DAYTONA International Speedway is a track like no other on the NASCAR circuit—a 2.5-mile-round, high-banked shrine to speed that requires power under the hood; a smooth, aerodynamic body; and the proper chassis-and-shock packages. The Daytona 500 is a challenge for the crews, especially since they've been away from racing for months. On most race weekends crews arrive at the track two days before the race; at Daytona the haulers enter the garage 10 days before the green flag drops. Speedweeks gives crew members time to shake off the rust and also to constantly adjust their cars and try out new setups; the 125-mile qualifying races serve as a prelim to the main event.

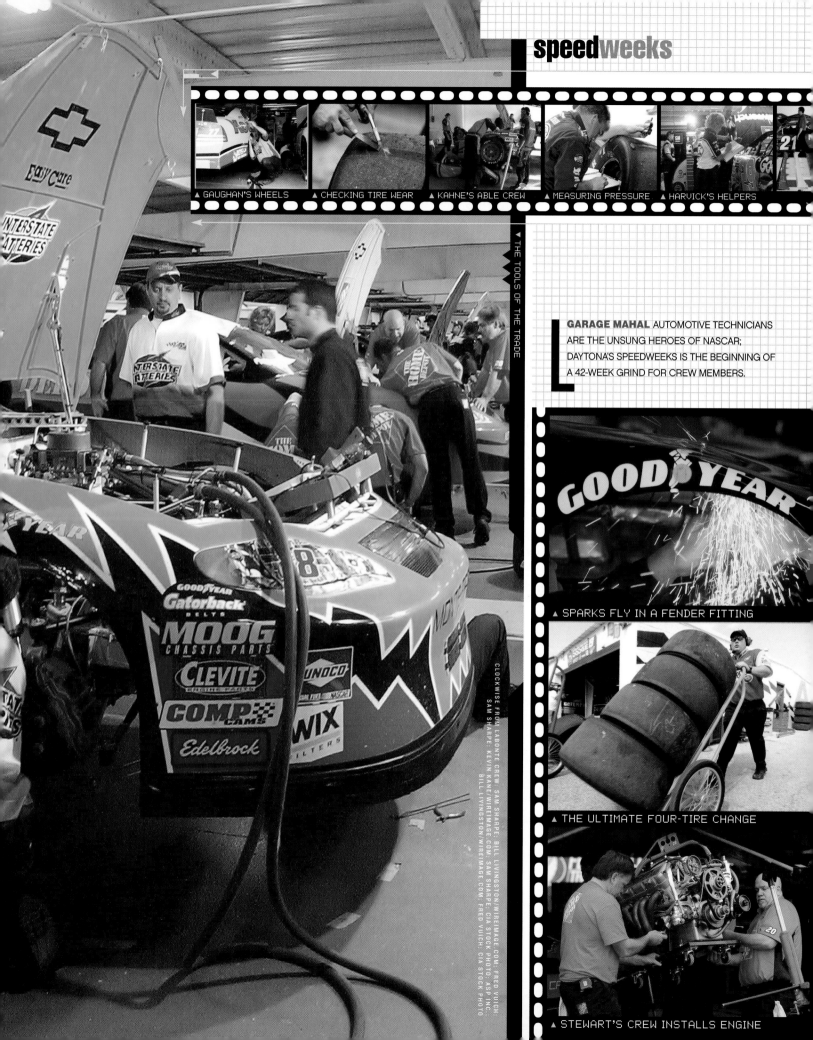

▲ GAUGHAN'S WHEELS ▲ CHECKING TIRE WEAR ▲ KAHNE'S ABLE CREW ▲ MEASURING PRESSURE ▲ HARVICK'S HELPERS

▼ THE TOOLS OF THE TRADE

GARAGE MAHAL AUTOMOTIVE TECHNICIANS ARE THE UNSUNG HEROES OF NASCAR; DAYTONA'S SPEEDWEEKS IS THE BEGINNING OF A 42-WEEK GRIND FOR CREW MEMBERS.

▲ SPARKS FLY IN A FENDER FITTING

▲ THE ULTIMATE FOUR-TIRE CHANGE

▲ STEWART'S CREW INSTALLS ENGINE

CLOCKWISE FROM: LABONTE CREW: SAM SHARPE; BILL LIVINGSTON/WIREIMAGE.COM; FRED VUICH; SAM SHARPE; KEVIN KANE/WIREIMAGE.COM; SAM SHARPE; CIA STOCK PHOTO; ASP INC.; BILL LIVINGSTON/WIREIMAGE.COM; FRED VUICH; CIA STOCK PHOTO

speedweeks

▲ TRUCK SERIES ACTION   ◆ SADLER WINS 125 RACE   ▲ THE 500 STARTS   ▲ JARRETT DELIVERS   ◆ KEEP ON TRUCKIN'

NONSTOP ACTION SPEEDWEEKS FEATURES 10 RACES OVER 16 DAYS, INCLUDING THE BUSCH AND THE CRAFTSMAN SERIES, AND, OF COURSE, THE DAYTONA 500.

THE IROC RACE MATCHES THE BEST FROM DIFFERENT SERIES ▶

▲ RAIN PUSHES BACK THE BUSCH RACE

▲ GUYS IN THE PITS TAKE SOME HITS

CLOCKWISE FROM IROC RACE: TOM RAYMOND: SAM SHARPE: CIA STOCK PHOTO: DOUG MURRAY/REUTERS; PETER COSGROVE/AP: GLENN SMITH/AP: FRED VUICH: SAM SHARPE: GEORGE TIEDEMANN/GT IMAGES: ASP ING: GLENN SMITH/AP

RACE DAYS

Make It a W for E

THERE'S NO PLACE a driver would rather visit than Victory
Lane at Daytona International Speedway—and they have plenty
of chances to get there. There's so much racing at Daytona that
by the time Dale Earnhardt memorably broke his 0-for-19 slump
in the 1998 Daytona 500, he had already won 30 races on the
track. In 2003 his son Dale Jr. nearly became the first driver to
win four races during one Speedweeks when he won the Bud
Shootout, his 125-mile qualifying race and the Busch race. The
following year Little E added NASCAR's most-coveted trophy to
his case, and he repeated his qualifying race and Busch Series
wins for good measure.

GO

2005
SEASON PREVIEW

From Daytona to Homestead: 36 races, 12,518 laps and a million thrills. Here's your guide to the greatest ride in sports

Compiled by Mark Lelinwalla
Race analysis by Lars Anderson

DAYTONA DAZE
PRACTICE LAPS
WERE A BLUR FOR
SCOTT RIGGS
AND KEN SCHRADER
DURING THE
RUN-UP TO THE
2004 DAYTONA 500.

PHOTOGRAPH BY
FRED VUICH

NEXTEL CUP 2005
RACE-BY-RACE CALENDAR

february

RACE 1
DAYTONA 500

FEB. 20, 2005 NETWORK: FOX
DAYTONA INTERNATIONAL SPEEDWAY
DAYTONA BEACH, FLA.

2004 WINNER: Dale Earnhardt Jr.

FIRST RACE: Feb. 22, 1959

WINNER: Lee Petty

QUALIFYING RECORD: Bill Elliott
210.364 mph, Feb. 9, 1987

RACE RECORD: Buddy Baker
177.602 mph, Feb. 17, 1980

MOST WINS: 7, Richard Petty

TRACK SPECS: 2.5-mile tri-oval, Turns 1–4
banked 31 degrees, tri-oval banked 18 degrees

IF YOU'RE GOING: Daytona USA, near Turn 4,
includes a variety of hands-on activities, three
motion-simulator rides and an IMAX theater,
which shows a 3-D NASCAR film.

TRACK CONTACT INFO: (386) 253-7223,
www.daytonaintlspeedway.com

INSIDE LINE: *The superspeedway
strength of DEI and Hendrick
Motorsports, whose teams swept the
four restrictor-plate races in '04,
means a driver from one of those
teams is likely to win this year's 500.*

RACE 2
AUTO CLUB 500

FEB. 27, 2005 NETWORK: FOX
CALIFORNIA SPEEDWAY
FONTANA, CALIF.

2004 WINNER: Jeff Gordon

FIRST RACE: June 22, 1997

WINNER: Jeff Gordon

QUALIFYING RECORD: Ryan Newman
187.432 mph, April 26, 2002

RACE RECORD: Jeff Gordon
155.012 mph, June 22, 1997

MOST WINS: 3, Jeff Gordon

TRACK SPECS: 2.0-mile oval, Turns 1–4
banked 14 degrees

IF YOU'RE GOING: Attend the Walk of Fame
induction ceremony on Friday, Feb. 25, when
the previous year's race winner will stamp his
footprints in concrete.

TRACK CONTACT INFO: (800) 944-RACE,
www.californiaspeedway.com

INSIDE LINE: *Racing at Fontana,
birthplace of the Hell's Angels, is
rugged; the wide track guarantees
plenty of side-by-side action. Look
for Kasey Kahne to get the first
victory of his young career.*

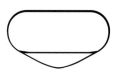

RACE 3

UAW-DAIMLERCHRYSLER 400

MARCH 13, 2005   NETWORK: FOX
LAS VEGAS MOTOR SPEEDWAY
LAS VEGAS, NEV.

2004 WINNER: Matt Kenseth

FIRST RACE: March 1, 1998

WINNER: Mark Martin

QUALIFYING RECORD: Kasey Kahne
174.904 mph, March 7, 2004

RACE RECORD: Mark Martin
146.554 mph, March 1, 1998

MOST WINS: 2, Jeff Burton, Matt Kenseth

TRACK SPECS: 1.5-mile oval, Turns 1–4
banked 12 degrees

IF YOU'RE GOING: After watching the race,
get behind the wheel yourself. The speedway is
home to the Richard Petty Driving Experience
(which also holds events at 16 other tracks).

TRACK CONTACT INFO: (800) 644-4444,
www.lvms.com

INSIDE LINE: *Matt Kenseth has won
the last two years at Las Vegas, but
keep an eye on Kurt Busch. The
Sin City native loves racing in front
of his friends, making this one of
the most important races for Busch.*

RACE 4

GOLDEN CORRAL 500

MARCH 20, 2005   NETWORK: FOX
ATLANTA MOTOR SPEEDWAY
HAMPTON, GA.

2004 WINNER: Dale Earnhardt Jr.

FIRST RACE: July 31, 1960

WINNER: Fireball Roberts

QUALIFYING RECORD: Bobby Labonte
194.957 mph, March 12, 1999

RACE RECORD: Dale Earnhardt
161.298 mph, March 10, 1996

MOST WINS: 6, Cale Yarborough

TRACK SPECS: 1.54-mile oval, Turns 1–4
banked 24 degrees

IF YOU'RE GOING: Trackside camping costs
$2,000 for four tickets (good Friday–Sunday)
and includes six guest passes (race day only) for
friends to watch the race from your RV.

TRACK CONTACT INFO: (770) 946-4211,
www.atlantamotorspeedway.com

INSIDE LINE: *Dale Earnhardt won
nine times here, and his son must
have been paying attention: Junior
has the highest average finish
(10.2) among active drivers with
at least five starts here.*

CRAFTSMAN

LAS VEGAS

JERR-DAN

UAW-DaimlerChrysler

RACE 5
FOOD CITY 500

APRIL 3, 2005   NETWORK: FOX
BRISTOL MOTOR SPEEDWAY
BRISTOL, TENN.

2004 WINNER: Kurt Busch

FIRST RACE: July 30, 1961

WINNER: Jack Smith

QUALIFYING RECORD: Ryan Newman
128.709 mph, March 23, 2003

RACE RECORD: Cale Yarborough
100.989 mph, April 17, 1977

MOST WINS: 6, Rusty Wallace

TRACK SPECS: .533-mile oval, Turns 1–4
banked 36 degrees

IF YOU'RE GOING: The Bristol YWCA offers
race-day child care from 10 a.m. to 8 p.m. for
youngsters 2–12. Preregistration is required
(call 423-968-9444), and the cost is $100.

TRACK CONTACT INFO: (423) 764-1161,
www.bristolmotorspeedway.com

INSIDE LINE: *This track is usually
tamed by a driver who's aggressive,
well-conditioned and likes to take
chances. That makes it Kurt Busch's
race to lose—and he has won four of
his last six starts here.*

RACE 6
ADVANCE AUTO PARTS 500

APRIL 10, 2005   NETWORK: FOX
MARTINSVILLE SPEEDWAY
MARTINSVILLE, VA.

2004 WINNER: Rusty Wallace

FIRST RACE: September 25, 1949

WINNER: Red Bryon

QUALIFYING RECORD: Jeff Gordon
94.307 mph, April 11, 2003

RACE RECORD: Rusty Wallace
81.410 mph, April 21, 1996

MOST WINS: 9, Richard Petty

TRACK SPECS: .526-mile oval, Turns 1–4
banked 12 degrees

IF YOU'RE GOING: No one is sure what's in
them, but the hot dogs from Martinsville
concession stands are legendary with fans and
drivers. More than 100,000 were sold during
last year's race, and Little E has been known to
scarf down a few as a prequalifying snack.

TRACK CONTACT INFO: (877)-RACE-TIX,
www.martinsvillespeedway.com

INSIDE LINE: *Cars tend to bunch up
around this short track, so drivers
with a knack for finding holes in
tight spaces (including Jeff Gordon
and Matt Kenseth) have the edge.*

REFLECTIONS
BOBBY LABONTE
AND CREW SHINE AT
MARTINSVILLE'S
ADVANCE 500: BOBBY
WON THERE IN '02
AND WAS SECOND
IN '03 AND '04.

PHOTOGRAPH BY
FRED VUICH

april

RACE 7
SAMSUNG/RADIO SHACK 500
APRIL 17, 2005   NETWORK: FOX
TEXAS MOTOR SPEEDWAY
JUSTIN, TEXAS

2004 WINNER: Elliott Sadler

FIRST RACE: April 6, 1997

WINNER: Jeff Burton

QUALIFYING RECORD: Bill Elliott

194.224 mph, April 5, 2002

RACE RECORD: Terry Labonte

144.276 mph, March 28, 1999

MOST WINS: 1, Jeff Burton, Mark Martin, Terry Labonte, Dale Earnhardt Jr., Dale Jarrett, Matt Kenseth, Ryan Newman, Elliot Sadler

TRACK SPECS: 1.5-mile oval, Turns 1–4 banked 24 degrees

IF YOU'RE GOING: Catch a cattle drive at the Fort Worth Stockyards, reenacted daily at 11:30 a.m. and 4 p.m. There's no charge for the show, and if you stick around, there's often live music down the street at Billy Bob's Texas, billed as the world's largest honky-tonk.

TRACK CONTACT INFO: (817) 215-8500, www.texasmotorspeedway.com

INSIDE LINE: *Eight drivers have won in eight years of racing at TMS. Look for a middle-of-the-pack driver like Ricky Rudd to make it nine.*

RACE 8
ARIZONA 500
APRIL 23, 2005   NETWORK: FOX
PHOENIX INTERNATIONAL RACEWAY
PHOENIX, ARIZ.

2004 WINNER: New race

FIRST RACE: Nov. 6, 1988

WINNER: Alan Kulwicki

QUALIFYING RECORD: Ryan Newman 135.854 mph, Nov. 5, 2004

RACE RECORD: Tony Stewart 118.132 mph, Nov. 7, 1999

MOST WINS: 2, Davey Allison, Jeff Burton, Dale Earnhardt Jr.

TRACK SPECS: 1.0-mile oval, Turns 1–2 banked 11 degrees, Turns 3–4 banked 9 degrees

IF YOU'RE GOING: Take a hike! The raceway sits at the base of the Estrella Mountains, which have 33 miles of hiking and biking trails.

TRACK CONTACT INFO: (866) 408-RACE, www.phoenixintlraceway.com

INSIDE LINE: *With its dogleg on the backstretch and uneven corners, PIR is a challenge for crew chiefs. Jeff Burton found the right formula in '00 and '01, so he's the one to watch.*

RACE 9
AARON'S 499
MAY 1, 2005   NETWORK: FOX
TALLADEGA SUPERSPEEDWAY
TALLADEGA, ALA.

2004 WINNER: Jeff Gordon

FIRST RACE: Sept. 14, 1969

WINNER: Richard Brickhouse

QUALIFYING RECORD: Bill Elliott
212.809 mph, April 30, 1987

RACE RECORD: Mark Martin
188.354 mph, May 10, 1997

MOST WINS: 3, David Pearson, Buddy Baker, Bobby Allison, Davey Allison, Dale Earnhardt

TRACK SPECS: 2.66-mile tri-oval, Turns 1–4 banked 33 degrees, tri-oval banked 18 degrees

IF YOU'RE GOING: Pay a visit to the International Motorsports Hall of Fame (next to the track) to see the Bud rocket car, unofficially the first car to break the sound barrier.

TRACK CONTACT INFO: (877) GO2-DEGA, www.talladegasuperspeedway.com

INSIDE LINE: *If Dale Earnhardt Jr. doesn't win this race, consider it an upset. He has been more dominant at Talladega (five wins in his last seven starts) than any other driver.*

RACE 10
CAROLINA DODGE DEALERS 500
MAY 7, 2005   NETWORK: FOX
DARLINGTON RACEWAY
DARLINGTON, S.C.

2004 WINNER: Jimmie Johnson

FIRST RACE: Sept. 4, 1950

WINNER: Johnny Mantz

QUALIFYING RECORD: Ward Burton
173.797 mph, March 22, 1996

RACE RECORD: Dale Earnhardt
139.958 mph, March 28, 1993

MOST WINS: 7, David Pearson

TRACK SPECS: 1.366-mile oval, Turns 1–2 banked 25 degrees, Turns 3–4 banked 23 degrees

IF YOU'RE GOING: You can get married in Victory Lane. A $200 fee covers the ceremony, pit passes and a gift from the track.

CONTACT INFO: (843) 395-8499, www.darlingtonraceway.com

INSIDE LINE: *Darlington will host a night race for the first time in its 55-year history. Veterans who are familiar with the track tend to do well, so keep an eye on Terry Labonte and Sterling Marlin.*

IN THE CLOUDS
DALE EARNHARDT JR.
MADE A VICTORY BURNOUT
LOOK POSITIVELY
CELESTIAL AFTER THE
'04 CHEVY AMERICAN
REVOLUTION 400
AT RICHMOND.

PHOTOGRAPH BY
JONATHAN FERREY/GETTY IMAGES

RACE 11
CHEVY AMERICAN REVOLUTION 400
MAY 14, 2005   NETWORK: FX
RICHMOND INTERNATIONAL RACEWAY
RICHMOND, VA.

2004 WINNER: Dale Earnhardt Jr.

FIRST RACE: April 19, 1953

WINNER: Lee Petty

QUALIFYING RECORD: Brian Vickers
129.983 mph, May 15, 2004

RACE RECORD: Rusty Wallace
108.499 mph, March 2, 1997

MOST WINS: 6, Richard Petty

TRACK SPECS: .750-mile oval, Turns 1–4
banked 14 degrees

IF YOU'RE GOING: Take time to smell the
peonies or see the "Butterflies LIVE!" exhibit at
the Lewis Ginter Botanical Garden.

TRACK CONTACT INFO: (866) 455-RACE,
www.rir.com

INSIDE LINE: *Richmond is a
superspeedway disguised as a short
track, so a hard-charging daredevil
like Tony Stewart tends to do well
here. Look for him to get his fourth
Richmond win in 2005.*

RACE 12
COCA-COLA 600
MAY 29, 2005   NETWORK: FOX
LOWE'S MOTOR SPEEDWAY
CONCORD, N.C.

2004 WINNER: Jimmie Johnson

FIRST RACE: June 19, 1960

WINNER: Joe Lee Johnson

QUALIFYING RECORD: Jimmie Johnson
187.052 mph, May 30, 2004

RACE RECORD: Bobby Labonte
151.952 mph, May 28, 1995

MOST WINS: 5, Darrell Waltrip

TRACK SPECS: 1.5-mile oval, Turns 1–4
banked 24 degrees

IF YOU'RE GOING: Nearly 90% of NASCAR
teams are based less than two hours away by
car, and many are well worth a visit.

TRACK CONTACT INFO: (800) 455-FANS,
www.lowesmotorspeedway.com

INSIDE LINE: *Jimmie Johnson blew
away the field in '04, leading 334 of
the race's 400 laps. Expect Johnson's
crew chief, Chad Knaus, to use the
same setup—and he'll probably get
the same result.*

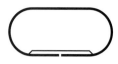

RACE 13
MBNA 400

JUNE 5, 2005   NETWORK: FX
DOVER INTERNATIONAL SPEEDWAY
DOVER, DEL.

2004 WINNER: Mark Martin

FIRST RACE: July 6, 1969

WINNER: Richard Petty

QUALIFYING RECORD: Jeremy Mayfield
161.522 mph, June 6, 2004

RACE RECORD: Bobby Labonte
120.603 mph, June 6, 1999

MOST WINS: 5, Bobby Allison

TRACK SPECS: 1.0-mile oval, Turns 1–4
banked 24 degrees

IF YOU'RE GOING: Log on to the track website
and try to win a seat in the luxurious new DuPont
Monster Bridge that's suspended 29 feet above
the track. Each seat has an amazing view plus
access to radio and TV race coverage.

TRACK CONTACT INFO: (800) 441-RACE,
www.doverspeedway.com

INSIDE LINE: *In 2004 teammates
Kasey Kahne and Jeremy Mayfield
were the class of the field before
getting caught up in wrecks. Their
luck should change in '05.*

RACE 14
POCONO 500

JUNE 12, 2005   NETWORK: FOX
POCONO RACEWAY
LONG POND, PA.

2004 WINNER: Jimmie Johnson

FIRST RACE: Aug. 5, 1974

WINNER: Richard Petty

QUALIFYING RECORD: Kasey Kahne
172.533 mph, June 13, 2004

RACE RECORD: Alan Kulwicki
144.023 mph, June 14, 1992

MOST WINS: 2, Jeff Gordon

TRACK SPECS: 2.5-mile oval, Turn 1 banked
14 degrees, Turn 2 banked 8 degrees, Turn 3
banked 6 degrees

IF YOU'RE GOING: Adventurous types can
take in the Pocono Mountains while kayaking or
rafting down the stunning Delaware River.
Adventure Sports (570-223-0505) is an
outfitter offering trips for all skill levels.

TRACK CONTACT INFO: (800) RACEWAY,
www.poconoraceway.com

INSIDE LINE: *Jimmie Johnson swept
both Pocono races in '04, so he's
the fave. But don't overlook his
teammates Jeff Gordon and
Brian Vickers.*

june

CAL CALL

JEFF GORDON (24)
CELEBRATED NASCAR'S
SECOND OF THREE 2004
STOPS IN HIS NATIVE
CALIFORNIA BY WINNING
THE 350-MILE ROAD
RACE AT SONOMA.

PHOTOGRAPH BY
ROBERT BECK

RACE 15
MICHIGAN 500
JUNE 19, 2005   NETWORK: FOX
MICHIGAN INTERNATIONAL SPEEDWAY
BROOKLYN, MICH.

2004 WINNER: Ryan Newman

FIRST RACE: June 15, 1969

WINNER: Cale Yarborough

QUALIFYING RECORD: Jeff Gordon
190.865 mph, June 20, 2004

RACE RECORD: Dale Jarrett
173.997 mph, June 13, 1999

MOST WINS: 6, Cale Yarborough

TRACK SPECS: 2.0-mile oval, Turns 1–4
banked 18 degrees

IF YOU'RE GOING: The Henry Ford Museum
in nearby Dearborn offers an impressive
collection of automotive and American history.

TRACK CONTACT INFO: (800) 354-1010,
www.mispeedway.com

INSIDE LINE: *Ford owners put extra
emphasis on this race because it's
in their company's backyard. Look
for a driver from the Roush stable—
our pick is Matt Kenseth—to
be celebrating in Victory Lane.*

RACE 16
DODGE/SAVE MART 350
JUNE 26, 2005   NETWORK: FOX
INFINEON RACEWAY
SONOMA, CALIF.

2004 WINNER: Jeff Gordon

FIRST RACE: June 11, 1989

WINNER: Ricky Rudd

QUALIFYING RECORD: Jeff Gordon
94.303 mph, June 27, 2004

RACE RECORD: Ricky Rudd
81.007 mph, June 23, 2002

MOST WINS: 4, Jeff Gordon

TRACK SPECS: 2.0-mile road course

IF YOU'RE GOING: Pay a visit to one of the
many wineries of Napa and Sonoma counties.
Short on time? Try the Viansa Winery and
Italian Marketplace adjacent to the track.

TRACK CONTACT INFO: (800) 870-RACE,
www.infineonraceway.com

INSIDE LINE: *This is Gordon
territory. Jeff Gordon has four
career wins at Infineon, and Robby
Gordon won in '03. If either falters,
road-course specialist Boris Said
could get his first Cup victory.*

RACE 17
PEPSI 400

JULY 2, 2005 **NETWORK: NBC**
DAYTONA INTERNATIONAL SPEEDWAY
DAYTONA BEACH, FLA.

2004 WINNER: Jeff Gordon

FIRST RACE: Feb. 22, 1959

WINNER: Lee Petty

QUALIFYING RECORD: Sterling Marlin
203.666 mph, July 3, 1986

RACE RECORD: Bobby Allison
173.473 mph, July 4, 1980

MOST WINS: 5, David Pearson

TRACK SPECS: 2.5-mile oval, Turns 1–4
banked 31 degrees, tri-oval banked 18 degrees

IF YOU'RE GOING: A Fan Zone pass ($85
online or by calling the track) provides garage
viewing and allows fans to sign their names on
the start-finish line.

TRACK CONTACT INFO: (386) 253-7223,
www.daytonaintlspeedway.com

INSIDE LINE: *Last year Jeff Gordon
used drafting help from Jimmie
Johnson to win this race and loosen
DEI's stranglehold on Daytona.
Look out for Tony Stewart, who had
two top five finishes here in '04.*

RACE 18
TROPICANA 400

JULY 10, 2005 **NETWORK: NBC**
CHICAGOLAND SPEEDWAY
JOLIET, ILL.

2004 WINNER: Tony Stewart

FIRST RACE: July 15, 2001

WINNER: Kevin Harvick

QUALIFYING RECORD: Jeff Gordon
186.942 mph, July 11, 2004

RACE RECORD: Kevin Harvick
136.832 mph, July 14, 2002

MOST WINS: 2, Kevin Harvick

TRACK SPECS: 1.5-mile tri-oval, Turns 1–4
banked 18 degrees

IF YOU'RE GOING: The Haunted Trails Family
Amusement center, a 15-minute drive from the
track, features roller coasters, two miniature
golf courses, go-karts and an arcade.

TRACK CONTACT INFO: (815) 727-RACE,
www.chicagolandspeedway.com

INSIDE LINE: *Recently, the track's
asphalt surface has gotten bumpier,
which means crew chiefs must pay
close attention to their cars' shock
absorbers. Kevin Harvick has won
here twice in three years.*

KID'S GRID

WHILE THE DRIVERS
NEGOTIATED POCONO'S
BANKED TURNS AND
SLINGSHOT STRAIGHTS,
AN ASPIRING YOUNG
CREW CHIEF PLOTTED
HIS OWN COURSE.

**PHOTOGRAPH BY
CIA STOCK PHOTO**

RACE 19
NEW ENGLAND 300
JULY 17, 2005 **NETWORK: TNT**
NEW HAMPSHIRE INTERNATIONAL
SPEEDWAY, LOUDON, N.H.

2004 WINNER: Kurt Busch

FIRST RACE: July 11, 1993

WINNER: Rusty Wallace

QUALIFYING RECORD: Ryan Newman
132.360 mph, July 23, 2004

RACE RECORD: Jeff Burton
117.134 mph, July 13, 1997

MOST WINS: 3, Jeff Burton

TRACK SPECS: 1.058-mile oval, Turns 1–4
banked 12 degrees

IF YOU'RE GOING: Make a weekend of it and
attend the annual Race Fever street festival in
nearby Concord on July 14. It's free!

TRACK CONTACT INFO: (603) 783-4931,
www.nhis.com

INSIDE LINE: *Because the long
straightaways allow cars to generate
speed, you'll see a lot of crashes
in the sharp turns. Kurt Busch
swept both races here last year, so
he's the guy to beat.*

RACE 20
PENNSYLVANIA 500
JULY 24, 2005 **NETWORK: TNT**
POCONO RACEWAY
LONG POND, PA.

2004 WINNER: Jimmie Johnson

FIRST RACE: Aug. 5, 1974

WINNER: Richard Petty

QUALIFYING RECORD: Tony Stewart
172.391 mph, July 21, 2000

RACE RECORD: Rusty Wallace
144.892 mph, July 21, 1996

MOST WINS: 4, Bill Elliott

TRACK SPECS: 2.5-mile oval, Turn 1 banked
14 degrees, Turn 2 banked 8 degrees, Turn 3
banked 6 degrees.

IF YOU'RE GOING: At the Midway, behind the
main grandstand, you'll find music, clowns,
jugglers and other free entertainment.

TRACK CONTACT INFO: (800) RACEWAY,
www.poconoraceway.com

INSIDE LINE: *"This is a long race to
sit through," Kevin Harvick says.
Rather than strategy, this will be a
battle of attrition. The most focused
driver with the most reliable
equipment will win.*

RACE 21
BRICKYARD 400

AUG. 7, 2005   NETWORK: NBC
INDIANAPOLIS MOTOR SPEEDWAY
INDIANAPOLIS

2004 WINNER: Jeff Gordon

FIRST RACE: Aug. 6, 1994

WINNER: Jeff Gordon

QUALIFYING RECORD: Casey Mears
186.293 mph, Aug. 8, 2004

RACE RECORD: Bobby Labonte
155.912 mph, Aug. 5, 2000

MOST WINS: 4, Jeff Gordon

TRACK SPECS: 2.5-mile oval, Turns 1–4
banked 9 degrees

IF YOU'RE GOING: The speedway is home to
an 18-hole golf course, with four of the holes
inside the track. The course ($90) is not open
on race weekend, so plan accordingly.

TRACK CONTACT INFO: (800) 822-4639,
www.brickyard400.com

INSIDE LINE: *Drivers love this race as
much as any on the calendar for one
reason: It's held at the tradition-rich
Brickyard. Jeff Gordon is clearly the
driver to beat; last year he won for a
record-tying fourth time at Indy.*

RACE 22
SIRIUS AT THE GLEN

AUG. 14, 2005   NETWORK: NBC
WATKINS GLEN INTERNATIONAL
WATKINS GLEN, N.Y.

2004 WINNER: Tony Stewart

FIRST RACE: Aug. 4, 1957

WINNER: Buck Baker

QUALIFYING RECORD: Jeff Gordon
124.580 mph, Aug. 8, 2003

RACE RECORD: Mark Martin
103.300 mph, Aug. 13, 1995

MOST WINS: 4, Jeff Gordon

TRACK SPECS: 2.45-mile road course, banks
range from 6 to 10 degrees

IF YOU'RE GOING: Adventurous families may
want to visit Watkins Glen State Park, where
nearly five miles of scenic hiking trails traverse
a breathtaking gorge and several waterfalls.

TRACK CONTACT INFO: (866) 461-RACE,
www.theglen.com

INSIDE LINE: *This road course
constantly fools drivers. Expect at
least six cars to fly off the track
because of excessive speed. Everyone
will be chasing Tony Stewart, who's
won here two of the last three years.*

BUMP IN THE NIGHT
THE EVENING RACE
AT BRISTOL ALWAYS
BRINGS FIREWORKS.
IN 2004 RICKY
RUDD (21) AND MIKE
WALLACE SPARKED
THINGS OFF.

RACE 23
GFS MARKETPLACE 400
AUG. 21, 2005   NETWORK: TNT
MICHIGAN INTERNATIONAL SPEEDWAY
BROOKLYN, MICH.

2004 WINNER: Greg Biffle

FIRST RACE: June 15, 1969

WINNER: Cale Yarborough

QUALIFYING RECORD: Dale Earnhardt Jr.
191.149 mph, Aug. 18, 2000

RACE RECORD: Bobby Labonte
157.739 mph, Aug. 20, 1995

MOST WINS: 5, David Pearson

TRACK SPECS: 2.0-mile oval, Turns 1–4
banked 18 degrees

IF YOU'RE GOING: Get close to the action by
buying a pit pass ($50). Fans can mingle with
racers and crews up until one hour before the
green flag drops.

TRACK CONTACT INFO: (800) 354-1010,
www.mispeedway.com

INSIDE LINE: *If Rusty Wallace is
going to win in his final year of
full-time Cup racing, it likely will
be here, where his five wins and 15
top five finishes lead all active
drivers.*

RACE 24
SHARPIE 500
AUG. 27, 2005   NETWORK: TNT
BRISTOL MOTOR SPEEDWAY
BRISTOL, TENN.

2004 WINNER: Dale Earnhardt Jr.

FIRST RACE: July 30, 1961

WINNER: Jack Smith

QUALIFYING RECORD: Jeff Gordon
128.520 mph, Aug. 27, 2004

RACE RECORD: Charlie Glotzbach
101.074 mph, July 11, 1971

MOST WINS: 7, Darrell Waltrip

TRACK SPECS: .533-mile oval, Turns 1–4
banked 36 degrees

IF YOU'RE GOING: At Bristol Caverns, eight
miles from the track, $9.50 ($5 for kids) gets
you a guided tour and a look at an underground
river and dazzling rock formations.

TRACK CONTACT INFO: (423) 764-6555,
www.bristolmotorspeedway.com

INSIDE LINE: *This is a spectacular
race to watch because it's at night
under the lights and the crowd is
right on top of the action. The key to
success is avoiding wrecks, which
Dale Earnhardt Jr. did in '04.*

RACE 25
LABOR DAY 500
SEPT. 4, 2005 NETWORK: NBC
CALIFORNIA SPEEDWAY
FONTANA, CALIF.

2004 WINNER: Elliott Sadler

FIRST RACE: June 22, 1997

WINNER: Jeff Gordon

QUALIFYING RECORD: Ryan Newman
187.432 mph, April 26, 2002

RACE RECORD: Jeff Gordon
155.012 mph, June 22, 1997

MOST WINS: 2, Jeff Gordon

TRACK SPECS: 2.0-mile oval, Turns 1–4
banked 14 degrees

IF YOU'RE GOING: NASCAR is a family sport,
so why not take your family on a trip to
Disneyland? The original home of Mickey is
about 50 miles from the track, in Anaheim.
Ticket and other info: disneyland.disney.go.com

TRACK CONTACT INFO: (800) 944-RACE,
www.californiaspeedway.com

INSIDE LINE: *Success at this track
requires a car with loads of
horsepower, so Ryan Newman's
Dodge could be a major factor.
Dodge and Ford cars took the top six
spots in last year's race.*

RACE 26
CHEVY ROCK AND ROLL 400
SEPT. 10, 2005 NETWORK: TNT
RICHMOND INTERNATIONAL RACEWAY
RICHMOND, VA.

2004 WINNER: Jeremy Mayfield

FIRST RACE: April 19, 1953

WINNER: Lee Petty

QUALIFYING RECORD: Ryan Newman
128.700 mph, Sept. 11, 2004

RACE RECORD: Dale Jarrett
109.047 mph, Sept. 6, 1997

MOST WINS: 6, Richard Petty

TRACK SPECS: .75-mile oval, Turns 1–4
banked 14 degrees

IF YOU'RE GOING: If shopping's your thing,
check out the Short Pump Town Center, a
1.2 million-square-foot open-air mall.

TRACK CONTACT INFO: (866) 455-RACE,
www.rir.com

INSIDE LINE: *You should see plenty
of paint-trading during this night
race as drivers make their final push
for the Chase. Dale Jarrett won here
in 1997 and '99, so keep your
binoculars on the UPS Ford.*

september

SERVICE INDUSTRY
JEFF GORDON'S CREW
WAS ALL BUSINESS AS
HE PULLED IN DURING
THE POP SECRET 500
AT FONTANA, BUT, ALAS,
GORDON'S ENGINE
BLEW ON LAP 209.

**PHOTOGRAPH BY
ROBERT BECK**

RACE 27
SYLVANIA 300
SEPT. 18, 2005 NETWORK: TNT
NEW HAMPSHIRE INTERNATIONAL
SPEEDWAY, LOUDON, N.H.

2004 WINNER: Kurt Busch

FIRST RACE: July 11, 1993

WINNER: Rusty Wallace

QUALIFYING RECORD: Ryan Newman
133.357 mph, Sept. 14, 2003

RACE RECORD: Jeff Gordon
112.078 mph, Aug. 28, 1998

MOST WINS: 2, Jeff Gordon

TRACK SPECS: 1.058-mile oval, Turns 1–4
banked 12 degrees

IF YOU'RE GOING: For a change of pace, how
about a visit to the Canterbury Shaker Village,
an internationally known museum with 25
original Shaker buildings?

TRACK CONTACT INFO: (603) 783-4931,
www.nhis.com

INSIDE LINE: *The Chase begins here.
That means you can expect the
contending drivers to be more
cautious, which could create an
opportunity for a driver such as Joe
Nemechek to reach Victory Lane.*

RACE 28
MBNA 400
SEPT. 25, 2005 NETWORK: TNT
DOVER INTERNATIONAL SPEEDWAY
DOVER, DEL.

2004 WINNER: Ryan Newman

FIRST RACE: July 6, 1969

WINNER: Richard Petty

QUALIFYING RECORD: Rusty Wallace
159.964 mph, Sept. 24, 1999

RACE RECORD: Mark Martin
132.719 mph, Sept. 21, 1997

MOST WINS: 4, Richard Petty

TRACK SPECS: 1.0-mile oval, Turns 1–4
banked 24 degrees

IF YOU'RE GOING: Feeling lucky? If so, you
might want to try your hand at one of the 2,500
slot machines on track property.

TRACK CONTACT INFO: (800) 441-RACE,
www.doverspeedway.com

INSIDE LINE: *Roush Racing's Mark
Martin and Kurt Busch had great
success in the '04 Dover races, and
the team should be strong again this
time. Perhaps Roush rookie Carl
Edwards will get his first win.*

RACE 29
TALLADEGA 500

OCT. 2, 2005   NETWORK: NBC
TALLADEGA SUPERSPEEDWAY
TALLADEGA, ALA.

2004 WINNER: Dale Earnhardt Jr.

FIRST RACE: Sept. 14, 1969

WINNER: Richard Brickhouse

QUALIFYING RECORD: Bill Elliott
209.005 mph, July 24, 1986

RACE RECORD: Dale Earnhardt Jr.
183.665 mph, Oct. 6, 2002

MOST WINS: 7, Dale Earnhardt

TRACK SPECS: 2.66-mile tri-oval, Turns 1–4
banked 33 degrees, tri-oval banked 18 degrees

IF YOU'RE GOING: You can pay your respects
to an Alabama legend with a visit to the Davey
Allison Walkway at the Talladega-Texaco Walk
of Fame, eight miles from the track. The
walkway is made of bricks that were donated by
racing fans from around the world.

TRACK CONTACT INFO: (877) GO2-DEGA,
www.talladegasuperspeedway.com

INSIDE LINE: *The DEI and
Hendrick cars are the heavy
favorites in this restrictor-plate
race, but Tony Stewart or Ryan
Newman could pull off an upset.*

RACE 30
BANQUET 400

OCT. 9, 2005   NETWORK: NBC
KANSAS SPEEDWAY
KANSAS CITY, KANS.

2004 WINNER: Joe Nemechek

FIRST RACE: Sept. 30, 2001

WINNER: Jeff Gordon

QUALIFYING RECORD: Jimmie Johnson
180.373 mph, Oct. 3, 2003

RACE RECORD: Joe Nemechek
128.058 mph, Oct. 10, 2004

MOST WINS: 2, Jeff Gordon

TRACK SPECS: 1.5-mile tri-oval, Turns 1–4
banked 15 degrees

IF YOU'RE GOING: The Fan Walk area in the
Kansas infield allows access to the drivers and
a view of the inspection stations.

TRACK CONTACT INFO: (866) 460-RACE,
www.kansasspeedway.com

INSIDE LINE: *No team has figured
out this track yet, so the most
unlikely drivers can work their way
to the front. Last year, for example,
Joe Nemechek and Ricky Rudd
finished one-two.*

UP ON THE ROOF
SOMETIMES THE
BEST SEAT IN THE
HOUSE IS NO SEAT
AT ALL, AS THESE
UPSTANDING FANS
SHOWED AT LOWE'S
MOTOR SPEEDWAY.

**PHOTOGRAPH BY
CIA STOCK PHOTO**

october

RACE 31
UAW-GM QUALITY 500
OCT. 15, 2005 **NETWORK: NBC**
LOWE'S MOTOR SPEEDWAY
CONCORD, N.C.

2004 WINNER: Jimmie Johnson

FIRST RACE: June 19, 1960	WINNER: Joe Lee Johnson
QUALIFYING RECORD: Ryan Newman 188.877 mph, Oct. 16, 2004	RACE RECORD: Jeff Gordon 160.306 mph, Oct. 11, 1999

MOST WINS: 3, Bobby Allison, Cale Yarborough, Mark Martin

TRACK SPECS: 1.5-mile oval, Turns 1–4 banked 24 degrees

IF YOU'RE GOING: A trip to Charlotte wouldn't be complete without some wings, ribs or burgers at Quaker Steak & Lube, just down the road from the track.

TRACK CONTACT INFO: (800) 455-FANS, www.lowesmotorspeedway.com

INSIDE LINE: *Team Hendrick owns this track. Last year Jimmie Johnson swept both races at Lowe's, and his teammate Jeff Gordon finished second here in the fall. But the Hendrick supremacy on this rough, bumpy track might be fleeting, as most drivers consider Lowe's to be their home track, and no one wants to lose in front of the hometown crowd.*

RACE 32
SUBWAY 500
OCT. 23, 2005 **NETWORK: NBC**
MARTINSVILLE SPEEDWAY
MARTINSVILLE, VA.

2004 WINNER: Jimmie Johnson

FIRST RACE: Sept. 25, 1949	WINNER: Red Bryon
QUALIFYING RECORD: Ryan Newman 97.043 mph, Oct. 24, 2004	RACE RECORD: Jeff Gordon 82.223 mph, Sept. 22, 1996

MOST WINS: 6, Richard Petty, Darrell Waltrip

TRACK SPECS: .526-mile oval, Turns 1–4 banked 12 degrees

IF YOU'RE GOING: Brace yourself, because you're bound to be close to the action. Even the worst seat in the house is only 300 yards from the track.

TRACK CONTACT INFO: (877) RACE-TIX, www.martinsvillespeedway.com

INSIDE LINE: *Like Talladega, Martinsville is a wild card in the Chase. It's the only short track among the final 10 races, and if you're a title contender, you'd better be careful. Last year Dale Earnhardt Jr. got caught up in a wreck that caused him to finish 33rd, effectively knocking him out of the championship hunt.*

RACE 33
BASS PRO SHOPS MBNA 500
OCT. 30, 2005 **NETWORK: NBC**
ATLANTA MOTOR SPEEDWAY
HAMPTON, GA.

2004 WINNER: Jimmie Johnson

FIRST RACE: July 31, 1960	WINNER: Fireball Roberts
QUALIFYING RECORD: Geoffrey Bodine 197.478 mph, Nov. 15, 1997	RACE RECORD: Dale Earnhardt 163.633 mph, Nov. 12, 1995

MOST WINS: 4, Richard Petty, Dale Earnhardt, Bobby Labonte

TRACK SPECS: 1.54-mile oval, Turns 1–4 banked 24 degrees

IF YOU'RE GOING: The First Baptist Church of Hampton offers Sunday service before the race in three tents on the front- and backstretches and in the infield.

TRACK CONTACT INFO: (770) 946-4211, www.atlantamotorspeedway.com

INSIDE LINE: *Atlanta is the fastest non-restrictor-plate track on the circuit, and familiar names from the Roush, Hendrick and DEI teams have run strongly here in the past. A dark horse could be Evernham Motorsports's Kasey Kahne. In his first year of Cup racing Kahne had two top five finishes at Atlanta. Look for an even stronger finish now that he's turned some laps in the number 9 car.*

RACE 34
LONE STAR 500
NOV. 6, 2005 **NETWORK: NBC**
TEXAS MOTOR SPEEDWAY
JUSTIN, TEXAS

2004 WINNER: New race

FIRST RACE: April 6, 1997	**WINNER:** Jeff Burton
QUALIFYING RECORD: Bill Elliott 194.224 mph, April 5, 2002	**RACE RECORD:** Terry Labonte 144.276 mph, March 28, 1999

MOST WINS: 1, Jeff Burton, Mark Martin, Terry Labonte, Dale Earnhardt Jr., Dale Jarrett, Matt Kenseth, Ryan Newman, Elliott Sadler

TRACK SPECS: 1.5-mile oval, Turns 1–4 banked 24 degrees

IF YOU'RE GOING: Don't pass up the chance to visit the Texas Cowboy Hall of Fame, which honors men and women who have excelled in rodeo and cutting. The museum (Barn A, Fort Worth Stockyards) includes a collection of antique wagons, carriages and sleighs.

TRACK CONTACT INFO: (817) 215-8500, www.texasmotorspeedway.com

INSIDE LINE: *In May, NASCAR awarded the track a second Cup race and scheduled it during the homestretch of the Chase. This should favor the Roush and Yates cars; those teams have performed the best at Texas over the last four seasons.*

RACE 35
CHECKER AUTO PARTS 500
NOV. 13, 2005 **NETWORK: NBC**
PHOENIX INTERNATIONAL RACEWAY
PHOENIX, ARIZ.

2004 WINNER: Dale Earnhardt Jr.

FIRST RACE: Nov. 6, 1988	**WINNER:** Alan Kulwicki
QUALIFYING RECORD: Ryan Newman 135.854 mph, Nov. 5, 2004	**RACE RECORD:** Tony Stewart 118.132 mph, Nov. 7, 1999

MOST WINS: 2, Davey Allison, Jeff Burton, Dale Earnhardt Jr.

TRACK SPECS: 1.0-mile oval, Turns 1–2 banked 11 degrees, Turns 3–4 banked 9 degrees

IF YOU'RE GOING: Explore the Monkey Village or the Wallaby Walkabout at the Phoenix Zoo (admission is $12 for adults, $5 for children 3–12), about 15 miles from the track. With more than 1,200 animals on exhibit and 2½ miles of walking trails, the zoo has something for everyone in the family.

TRACK CONTACT INFO: (866) 408-RACE, www.phoenixintlraceway.com

INSIDE LINE: *Phoenix is a driver's track. Handling is more crucial than anything else here, and that usually gives the edge to the drivers who have the best car control. Because of this, keep a close eye on Matt Kenseth, Ryan Newman and Kasey Kahne.*

RACE 36
FORD 400
NOV. 20, 2005 **NETWORK: NBC**
HOMESTEAD-MIAMI SPEEDWAY
HOMESTEAD, FLA.

2004 WINNER: Greg Biffle

FIRST RACE: Nov. 14, 1999	**WINNER:** Tony Stewart
QUALIFYING RECORD: Jamie McMurray 181.111 mph, Nov. 14, 2003	**RACE RECORD:** Bobby Labonte 116.868 mph, Nov. 16, 2003

MOST WINS: 2, Tony Stewart

TRACK SPECS: 1.5-mile oval, Turns 1–4 banked 18 to 20 degrees

IF YOU'RE GOING: Plan to attend the Ford Racefest, which will take place on Nov. 18 in downtown Fort Lauderdale from noon to 10 p.m. In addition to live music and other entertainment, Ford drivers will be on hand to sign autographs for fans.

TRACK CONTACT INFO: (800) 409-RACE, www.homesteadmiamispeedway.com

INSIDE LINE: *There will be fireworks at Homestead. The championship wraps up here, so count on plenty of bumping and banging among the leaders. Who does this track favor? Whoever wants it most. We predict, however, that Jeff Gordon will hoist the trophy as the 2005 Nextel Cup champion.*

THE future IS NOW

You could wait for the Chase—or you could turn the page and find out what the Great DW sees in store for the '05 Nextel Cup season **by Darrell Waltrip**

1. Kurt Busch won't win back-to-back Nextel Cup titles . . . **probably.**

RECENT HISTORY HAS SHOWN THAT it's not easy to repeat; the last to do it was Jeff Gordon in 1997 and '98. Look at what happened to 2003 champion Matt Kenseth. He came out of the gate smokin' in '04, taking the checkered flag in two of the first three races. He wanted to prove to everybody that he was a worthy champion, and he was terrific for the first month. But then we never heard from Matt again because he had so many back-of-the-pack finishes. (Twelve times he ended up 20th or worse, compared with five such finishes in '03.) Off the track, every week it seems as if there are 100 people pulling a defending champion in 100 different

season Ford got a new nose and tail, which helped make its cars better aerodynamically. And remember, the Roush-Yates engine alliance was formed before last season, and that gave both teams more horsepower. Busch still has these things going for him as he dives into 2005. Another thing working in his favor is that he races well on all kinds of tracks. Even though history says otherwise, I wouldn't be surprised if Busch is the driver who bucks the recent trend of champions not repeating.

2. The biggest surprise of 2005 will be . . . **Kasey Kahne.**

MARK MY WORDS: KASEY KAHNE IS THE next Jeff Gordon. I remember 1993, when Gordon was

L **THEY GOT NEXT . . . WE THINK** AS THE 2005 SEASON GETS ROLLING, ALL EYES—INCLUDING THOSE OF DARRELL WALTRIP—WILL BE ON (FROM LEFT)

directions, wanting him to do an appearance or an interview or a commercial shoot. On the track everybody but your teammates seems to be ganging up on you, and this can be exhausting. Sure, Matt qualified for the Chase, but he was a nonfactor in virtually all 10 races and finished the year eighth in the final standings. The moral of the story is this: It's so easy to lose your focus after winning the title.

That said, I have to admit that I really do like Busch's chances. After I won the title in 1981, I made sure that nothing changed. My crew chief, my team, heck, even my public relations guy all stayed the same—and that's why I won again in 1982. I can't stress enough how important it is to have continuity, and I think Kurt is smart enough to know and understand this. He'll do everything he can to make sure that title fever doesn't change him or his team.

Kurt also has been blessed with good timing. Before the 2004

a rookie and seemed to crash in every race. He was always fast, but he was always in trouble. In fact, when Rick Hendrick, Gordon's team owner, asked me what I thought about Jeff, I told him that Jeff would never succeed at the Cup level because he wrecked too much. Obviously I was wrong. Gordon quickly acquired what drivers call "the feel" of the race car. It's hard to explain, but the feel comes with experience—the kind of experience, for example, that tells you when something is going on with your right front tire. If you have the feel, you instinctively know when one of your front tires is going down and know that you'd better pit right away. Because if you stay on the track for an extra lap, your tire will go flat, you'll slam into the wall, and your day will be over. Kasey learned this the hard way on several occasions last year, and you can be sure he won't make the same mistakes in '05.

And with a year of Cup racing under his belt, Kasey (like Gordon) will communicate better with his crew chief, Tommy

Baldwin Jr. In turn, Tommy will begin to trust his young driver more. I see Kasey winning at least once this season and qualifying for the Chase.

The Rookie of the Year will be ... Kyle Busch.

WATCHING KYLE IN THE BUSCH SERIES last year, I was struck by how aggressive he could be and still get away with it. Just like his older brother Kurt, he's reckless, he has no fear, he never gives up and he always seems to be near the front of the pack at the end of the race. Kyle will be driving for Hendrick Motorsports, which means he will have superior equipment and excellent guidance. So take this to the bank: Young Mr. Busch will blow away the rest of the rookies in the field.

cannot compete with the younger guys in our sport anymore. When the older drivers start a race, they tell themselves, "I've got 500 laps, no need to hurry. Take care of my equipment. Let the race come to me."

Problem is, races don't come to drivers anymore. The kids in the sport are going full-out as soon as the green flag drops. The older driver simply can't imagine how hard he has to push himself—and his car—for all 500 laps. And racing is just like any other sport in that 45-year-olds can't keep up with 23-year-olds. A good analogy is golf. I'm 58 years old, and the other day I played 18 holes and was dead tired when I walked off the last green. But a young kid will be chomping at the bit to go out and play 36 more holes.

Terry, Mark and Rusty have a tall hill to climb to be successful in '05, but I think one of them will do it. And boy, it sure would be heartwarming.

DEFENDING NEXTEL CUP CHAMPION KURT BUSCH AND HIS QUEST TO REPEAT, UP-AND-COMER KAHNE, ROOKIE KYLE BUSCH AND THE SOON-TO-RETIRE WALLACE.

The feel-good story of 2005 will be ... the last hurrahs of Terry Labonte, Mark Martin and Rusty Wallace.

EVERYBODY IN THE SPORT WOULD LOVE TO SEE THIS fraternity of fortysomethings (all of whom are retiring from full-time Cup racing at the end of '05) go out with at least one victory each. We want them to do something dramatic, and they're all still capable. I suspect one of them will make a splash at some point in the season. Perhaps one will even sneak into the Chase for the Championship.

But here's a cold, hard fact: Older guys just

The next big change NASCAR makes will be ... the introduction of a new (or is that old?) car.

NASCAR IS QUIETLY DEVELOPING A NEW CAR AT ITS research and development center in Concord, N.C. The car will have a slightly different look; it'll be what I call a "Back to the Future" car. It'll basically be the same big car that we raced in the '80s but with several refinements. The major thing is that this car will be less aero-dependent than today's. This new car, which NASCAR could unveil by the end of the year, will lessen the need for clean air. It'll also be safer, which is always a good thing. □

HOW SI RANKS THE DRIVERS

1. Jeff **GORDON**
2. Jimmie **JOHNSON**
3. Dale **EARNHARDT JR.**
4. Tony **STEWART**
5. Kurt **BUSCH**
6. Matt **KENSETH**
7. Elliott **SADLER**
8. Kasey **KAHNE**
9. Kevin **HARVICK**
10. Ryan **NEWMAN**
11. Jamie **MCMURRAY**
12. Mark **MARTIN**
13. Jeremy **MAYFIELD**
14. Dale **JARRETT**
15. Bobby **LABONTE**
16. Brian **VICKERS**
17. Carl **EDWARDS**
18. Jeff **BURTON**
19. Greg **BIFFLE**
20. Scott **RIGGS**

GIVE HIM FIVE
AT 33 JEFF GORDON STILL HAS ENOUGH FIREPOWER TO STOP THE YOUNG GUNS AND TAKE A FIFTH CHAMPIONSHIP.

PHOTOGRAPH BY
NIGEL KINRADE

2005 SCOUTING REPORTS

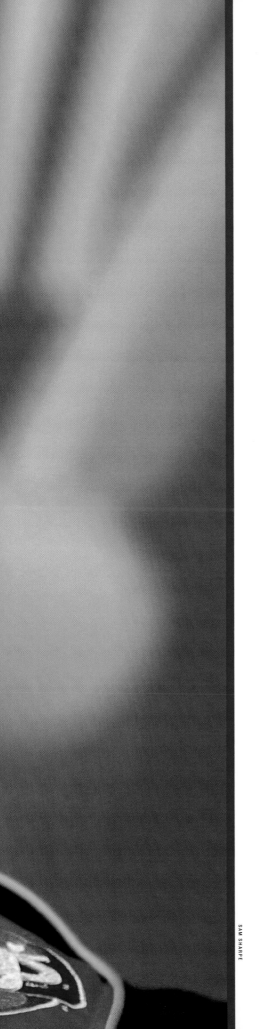

JEFF GORDON LAUGHED AT THE QUESTION, AS IF he'd just heard a rib-tickling one-liner at a roast in his honor. As Gordon sat in his team's hauler at Bristol Motor Speedway on Aug. 26, with the Sharpie 500 two days away, he was asked if he's a better driver now, at age 33, than he was in his 20s, when he won three championships between 1995 and '98.

"What, you think I'm over the hill?" Gordon said between guffaws. "I mean, I sure hope I'm better. I've certainly got more experience, and I think I make better decisions on the racetrack. Heck, I think I'm just starting to hit my prime."

In 2004 Gordon certainly drove like it. How impressive was the (aging) Kid? He led the Nextel Cup in top 10 finishes with 25, he had five wins (only Jimmie Johnson, with eight, and Dale Earnhardt Jr., with six, had more) and he took six poles (second only to Ryan Newman, who had nine). In the Chase for the Championship he was in contention right to the final lap of the final race, winding up third, just 16 points behind champion Kurt Busch. It's worth noting that under the old points system, Gordon would have taken his fifth title.

"The amazing thing about Jeff is that he rarely makes a mistake, and he always gets the most out of the car," says Gordon's crew chief, Robbie Loomis. "There's a reason he's won as many championships as he has: He's damn good."

Gordon started 2004 slowly: After six races he was in 12th place in the point standings. He climbed into third after he won the Aaron's 499 at Talladega last April 25, which was a watershed victory for Gordon and Hendrick Motorsports. Until that event Gordon hadn't taken the checkered flag at a superspeedway since 2000, when he won the Diehard 500 at Talladega. During that winless streak Gordon was the first to admit that Hendrick had fallen behind Dale Earnhardt Inc. in its restrictor-plate racing program. (Between 2001 and '03 DEI drivers Earnhardt Jr. and Michael Waltrip won nine of the 12 restrictor-plate races.) Yet last season Gordon followed up his spring Talladega victory with an even more impressive performance at Daytona's Pepsi 400 on July 3, when he became the first driver since Cale Yarborough in 1981 to win that race from the pole. More significant, Gordon's victory signaled the end of DEI's restrictor-plate hegemony and now makes Gordon an early favorite for the '05 Daytona 500.

"We were pretty sick of watching [DEI] play with us on the superspeedways," says Gordon. "They could pass when they wanted, lead when they wanted. It was embarrassing."

Can you hear the competitiveness in his voice? Gordon's teammate Johnson says he hears it every day. "Even though Jeff's been doing this a long time, trust me when I say he's not slowing down at all," Johnson says. "In reality, he's speeding up."

Which is why he's SI's pick to win it all in 2005.

—*Lars Anderson*

RUNS WELL AT: A history buff, Gordon is more driven to win at tradition-rich Indy than at any other track. Last season he made it to Victory Lane at the Brickyard for a record-tying fourth time.

TROUBLE SPOTS: There aren't any tracks at which Gordon can't win, but last year he blew an engine at both California Speedway and its sister two-mile track, Michigan International Speedway.

PROJECTION: Gordon appears to be reaching the prime of his career, which is a scary proposition for the rest of the Nextel Cup field.

FAST FACT
With 69 wins in his 12-year career, Gordon has 14 more victories than any other active NASCAR driver.

2 Jimmie JOHNSON

LAST SEASON: 6,498 POINTS, 2ND PLACE

IT BEGAN AT ATLANTA IN THE CHILL OF EARLY spring and ended at Pocono in the heat of midsummer. Over a stretch of 17 races, Jimmie Johnson seemed to leave a whirlwind in the wake of his Lowe's Chevrolet as he blew away the Nextel Cup field. In those 17 races he had 14 top 10 finishes, 13 top fives and four victories. So dominant was he that at one point he owned a 232-point lead in the standings, and had NASCAR not adopted its new Chase for the Championship playoff format, Johnson might have run away with the points title in even more overwhelming fashion than Matt Kenseth did in 2003.

"There was a time when we could do nothing wrong," says Johnson, a seasonlong critic of the Chase format. "But then the wheels came off."

After winning the Pennsylvania 500 on Aug. 1, Johnson, 29, suddenly slumped. Over the next six weeks he encountered engine problems and a stunning string of bad luck. He finished 36th or worse four times in those weeks, eroding both his points lead and the morale of his team as they entered the Chase.

"This sport is so humbling," Johnson says. "You can be on a tear and have a 232-point lead, but once Lady Luck changes on you a little bit, the momentum can drop in a hurry. It seemed once things started happening, they didn't stop for a while."

"Jimmie is a resilient guy," said Hendrick Motorsports teammate Jeff Gordon. "He'll come back."

Did he ever. After consecutive finishes of 37th and 32nd (the result of an overheated engine and an accident, respectively) dropped him to ninth only four weeks into the Chase, Johnson got hot again. He won on his sponsor's track at Lowe's Motor Speedway on Oct. 16, and the following week he won again, at Martinsville, to climb to fourth in the standings. That day turned tragic, though, when a plane carrying 10 members of the Hendrick Motorsports family crashed on its way to the track. All on board were killed, including owner Rick Hendrick's son, Ricky; his brother, John; his twin nieces, Jennifer and Kimberly; as well as the team's chief engine builder, Randy Dorton. Amid their grief, Johnson and his team rededicated themselves to the Chase. Johnson won for the third week in a row at Atlanta and again two weeks later at Darlington. In the end, though, it was not quite enough. A runner-up finish in the final race of the season at Homestead-Miami Speedway left him second in the standings, eight points behind Kurt Busch (who took fifth at Homestead).

"Jimmie had an amazing year," Busch said. "It's incredible that he was able to keep his focus even after the tragedy. He's just a great race driver."

There was no doubt of that in 2004. Now look for Johnson to prove it again in '05. —L.A.

RUNS WELL AT: Johnson and crew chief Chad Knaus have figured out Pocono. Last year they swept both races at the 2.5-mile oval, and they may do it again in 2005.

TROUBLE SPOTS: JJ is not a fan of Michigan International Speedway. In 2003 he crawled to a 27th-place finish, and last year an engine problem forced him to come home in 40th.

PROJECTION: After leading all drivers in victories last season with eight, Johnson is a star. He'll win multiple Cup titles in his career.

FAST FACT
Johnson has been in the top 10 in the standings for all but six weeks of the past three seasons.

NIGEL KINRADE

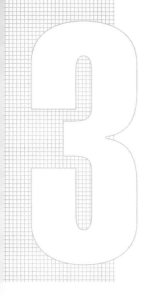

3

dale EARNHARDT jr.

LAST SEASON: 6,368 POINTS, 5TH PLACE

RELAXING BETWEEN PRACTICES AT TALLADEGA on Oct. 1, Dale Earnhardt Jr. lay on a couch in the back room of his team's hauler, a can of soda in his left hand. A television was on and several of his team members flitted in and out of the cramped room, but Junior didn't notice any of the activity; his mind was on the past.

Ten weeks had gone by since Little E had barely escaped a harrowing fire after crashing his Corvette during a warmup lap for an American Le Mans Series race in Sonoma, Calif., and the accident, which was the defining event of Earnhardt's 2004 season, was still in his thoughts. "The heat got up to over 1,000 degrees," said Junior, shaking his head as he described the crash moment by terrifying moment. "I was in the car for 14 seconds. I do feel that my dad [the late Dale Earnhardt Sr.] was with me. I heard someone holler, 'Come on! Come on! Get out!' Yet nobody was there. . . . Now it's time to move on."

Junior did just that. Two days later he won the EA 500 to temporarily grab the lead in the Chase for the Championship. (He would drop back to second two days later when NASCAR docked him 25 points, and fined him $10,000, for using profanity in his postrace interview on live television.) Though he would win again at the Checker Auto Parts 500 in Phoenix on Nov. 7, back-to-back 33rd-place finishes in the preceding weeks had cost him too many points, and he wound up fifth in the standings.

"I'm proud of my team," said Junior after finishing 23rd in the season's final race, the Ford 400 at Homestead-Miami Speedway. "We had good days and we had bad days, but we battled and put together our best season ever. We'll regroup in the off-season, and in 91 days we'll do it all over again."

Junior's 2004 season can be cleaved into two sections: preinjury and postinjury. Before he suffered second-degree burns on his legs and neck, Earnhardt consistently ran in the front of the pack, scoring three wins, nine top fives and only three 20th-or-worse finishes in 18 races. After he was hurt, Junior appeared to lose that get-the-hell-out-of-my-way determination that characterized his driving before the crash.

"You lose your edge after a serious accident," says three-time Cup champion Darrell Waltrip. "Every time you have a close call, you'll get a flashback."

Yet as Junior's burns got better, so too did his performance, which gives hope to his legion of fans for 2005. At age 30 Earnhardt has matured into a complete racer. Always strong on the superspeedways, he has also become NASCAR's best short-track racer; he scored more points on the short tracks in 2004 than any other driver. "Dale Jr. is as talented as any driver out there," says Matt Kenseth, "so there's no question he can win a championship."

The question is when.   —L.A.

RUNS WELL AT: Like his daddy, Junior loves restrictor-plate racing. In '04 he won two of the four plate races; this year look for him to take the checkered flag at least once at Daytona and Talladega.

TROUBLE SPOTS: California was not kind to Junior last year. Not only was the state the site of his fiery crash, but California Speedway also gave him fits: In his two starts there he was 19th and 34th.

PROJECTION: If Little E hadn't gotten hurt in 2004, he might have won the title. He'll be in the championship mix again this season.

FAST FACT

Junior won one title in '04—as an owner. Martin Truex Jr. took the Busch crown for Earnhardt's Chance 2 team.

tony STEWART

LAST SEASON: 6,326 POINTS, 6TH PLACE

THE LEARJET HAD JUST BROKEN THROUGH THE clouds at 20,000 feet over central Pennsylvania, and suddenly the summer sky was wide and blue. It was last July 31, and as Tony Stewart reclined and looked out the window, he began to try to explain why he believes he's the most misunderstood man in motor sports today.

"There are definitely two sides to me," said Stewart, the 2002 Winston Cup champion. "I'm not just the person that everybody reads about in the media. But I've made my bed, and I'm sleeping in it."

For much of the 2004 season that bed wasn't too comfortable, because Stewart, 33, was at the center of several controversies. The most obvious display of how highly revved his internal motor was came last June 27 at Infineon Raceway in Sonoma, Calif., when he tangled on the track with Brian Vickers (Vickers claimed Stewart hit his car early in the race, then later spun and wrecked him), who gave Stewart the one-fingered salute. Afterward, while Vickers sat in his car in the garage, an angry Stewart approached and cursed at the rookie. When Vickers laughed in response, Stewart hit him in the chest with an open palm, knocking the wind out of Vickers.

Vickers downplayed the incident, but NASCAR fined Stewart $50,000 and placed him on probation until Aug. 18. Other drivers were less forgiving of Stewart's aggressiveness on the track—Jamie McMurray called Stewart "an idiot," and Rusty Wallace said he wanted to "whip his rear end." Even owner Ray Evernham, after his driver Kasey Kahne was involved in a wreck with Stewart at Chicagoland Speedway on July 11, told reporters that he'd "like to have 10 minutes with Tony Stewart and handle [him] myself."

RUNS WELL AT: Stewart's open-wheel background has helped him become a road-course warrior. He's especially strong at Watkins Glen, where he has won two of the last three races.

TROUBLE SPOTS: In his last four starts at Bristol Motor Speedway, a track that saps the stamina of a driver faster than any on the circuit, Stewart has failed to finish higher than 19th.

PROJECTION: The '02 champ will continue to run near the front, but problems at Joe Gibbs Racing will keep him from the top spot.

> FAST FACT
> In November, Stewart purchased 50-year-old Eldora Speedway, a half-mile clay oval in Rossburg, Ohio.

"I'm a racer," Stewart says. "That's who I am. No one wants to win more than me, and when I make a mistake, it stays with me. If I was out of line, I'll let that person know. I'll apologize and be a man about it. But I won't apologize for racing hard. I always give my best effort, and I'll never be sorry for that."

Yet it wasn't Stewart's overzealousness that caused him to finish a disappointing sixth in the Chase for the Championship, despite winning two races. His big problem was that his Home Depot Chevrolet wasn't as consistently fast as the Chase leaders, which many in the garage believe is a reflection of an organizational problem at Joe Gibbs Racing. "The whole Gibbs operation needs to get its act together," says three-time Cup champion turned Fox television commentator Darrell Waltrip. "They seem to be slipping. That's why 2005 will be a key year for Tony Stewart."

"I know what it takes to win a championship," Stewart says. "And I'm 100 percent confident I'll get back to that level."

Will it be in 2005? Not likely. —L.A.

GEORGE TIEDEMANN/GT IMAGES

NO MATTER WHAT YOU THINK OF KURT BUSCH— and, judging by the thunder of boos he has long received before every race, it might not be very much—you've got to give him credit: He has done a lot of growing up in the last year. Busch is no longer the hotheaded, overly aggressive racer who earned the full-throated scorn of NASCAR fans in 2003. "I was forced to take a long look in the mirror at the end of last season and evaluate a lot of things," Busch says. "I'd like to think I've taken some positive steps in the right direction."

After Busch intentionally wrecked Jimmy Spencer in 2003 during a race at Michigan, prompting Spencer to punch him in the face in the garage afterward, Busch's owner, Jack Roush, ordered Busch to enter a mentoring program. He obliged, and in the off-season he met with several veteran drivers who tried to help him become a better citizen of NASCAR Nation. The mentoring seems to have transformed him, because in '04, his fourth season on the Cup circuit, the 26-year-old Las Vegas native was usually as well-behaved as any driver in the garage and rarely lost his cool—two factors that explain how Busch was able to drive off with the inaugural Nextel Cup.

"Kurt's matured," says Busch's crew chief, Jimmy Fennig. "He's got so much talent. Now he's applying it more. He's a little more patient now than he was in the beginning."

"Jack is a father figure to me," says Busch of Roush. "But he's also the boss. He provides the experience and cars, and I guess he looks at me for the youth and spunk."

Over the first 26 races of '04, Busch's youth was more apparent than his spunk. He had only one top five finish in his first 13 starts; he often made callow mistakes, like trying to squeeze through a hole that wasn't there; and he came into the Chase off a stretch in which he had failed to notch a top five finish in seven consecutive races. But once the green flag dropped on the playoff season, Busch became a different driver. He was patient, he avoided accidents, he conserved his engines, and he didn't make a single serious mistake in the first five races of the Chase. Subsequently he reeled off five straight top 10 finishes and, improbably, held the lead in the standings over Jimmie Johnson and Jeff Gordon going into the final race of the Chase, the Ford 400 at Homestead-Miami Speedway.

On Lap 93 of that race the wheels nearly came off Busch's title run—literally—when his right front wheel broke off his car as he was entering the pits. Amid a shower of sparks Busch dodged the barrier at the head of pit row by inches and limped into his pit. Driving with precision and control, he climbed back to finish fifth and clinch the Cup by eight points over Johnson.

"I plan on being in the sport for a long time," Busch says. "And hopefully I can win multiple championships."

After his performance in '04, that suddenly seems not just possible, but probable.   —L.A.

> **RUNS WELL AT:** Bristol suits the new champ's aggressive style; he has won there three times in the past two seasons. Busch has also made some loud noise in Loudon, winning both New Hampshire races in 2004.
>
> **TROUBLE SPOTS:** Chicagoland. Busch has pretty much been blown away in the Windy City, finishing 35th and 39th the past two years.
>
> **PROJECTION:** If Busch can stay out of trouble and continue to do what he did in '04, the victories and the championships will keep coming, and the boo-birds will eventually fly away.

FAST FACT
Busch was best when it mattered most—his average finish (8.9) was the best of any driver in the final 10 races.

WHAT'S GOTTEN INTO MATT KENSETH?

In 2003, as he cruised to his first Cup title, Kenseth was the least controversial, and perhaps least colorful, champion of the past decade. Competitors respected his clean racing; NASCAR officials considered him the Boy Scout of the garage; and fans marveled at how, even when he got bumped at 180 mph, he never let emotion cloud his judgment.

Then came 2004, when the 32-year-old native of Cambridge, Wis., showed that he isn't the boy next door after all. At Darlington last March, he argued heatedly with officials after he was assessed a one-lap penalty for passing under caution. A week later, at Bristol, Kenseth and Jamie McMurray twice traded paint, prompting Ganassi Racing team manager Andy Graves to say, "Matt comes across as the sweet, innocent type, but he's a lot dirtier driver than everybody thinks."

Three and a half months later, at Pocono, Kenseth engaged in his biggest dustup. During the final caution of the Pocono 500, as Kenseth appeared to slow, Kevin Harvick bumped into the back of the DeWalt Ford, and Kenseth spun out. After restarting his car, Kenseth bolted through the field and—still under caution— rammed Harvick, causing him to spin. "Matt needs to check his ego, because it's getting too big," Harvick said. (Both drivers were

RUNS WELL AT: The kid from Wisconsin runs well on all types of tracks, but he has been on a mini winning streak at Las Vegas, earning victories there in 2003 and '04.

TROUBLE SPOTS: Qualifying (his average starting spot in 2004 was 21.6) and superspeedways (Kenseth's average finish in restrictor-plate races in '04 was 26th).

PROJECTION: With his talent and consistency—and the Roush Fords' power—the '03 champ has a real shot at title number 2.

FAST FACT
A true green-and-gold Packers fan, Kenseth traded helmets with Green Bay QB Brett Favre.

penalized 10 finishing spots.) "I'm the same person I've always been," Kenseth says. "I haven't gone looking for [controversy]. It's just found me."

Kenseth won more races (two) in '04 than he did in his title season (one), but he knocked himself out of the Chase by crashing into a barrier on pit road at Dover. ("On the list of dumbest things I've done in a race car, this is tops," he said.) Nonetheless, Kenseth still possesses all the skills to win multiple championships, and pal Dale Earnhard Jr. says, "As long as Matt is in this sport, he'll be a contender. That boy is so good that he'll always be near the front." —L.A.

elliott SADLER

LAST SEASON: 6,024 POINTS, 9TH PLACE

ELLIOTT SADLER STOOD OUTSIDE a hospitality tent in the Daytona infield last February and made a prediction. The first race of the 2004 season, the Daytona 500, was still three days away, but Sadler was already sure of one thing: This was going to be his breakout year.

"I've never felt better about what I can accomplish before a season than I do right now," said Sadler, 29. "I really feel that we've got a chance to sneak up on some people."

Sadler, NASCAR's most improved driver last season, did just that. In 2003, his first season driving for owner Robert Yates, Sadler finished 22nd and appeared destined to spend his career as a middle-of-the-packer. But in '04 he was the most consistent racer on the circuit. He was not just the only driver to finish all 26 pre-Chase races, he was also the only one to qualify for the Chase after finishing out of the Top 20 the previous season.

RUNS WELL AT: Sadler has been a star in the Lone Star State, qualifying on the front row at Texas in 2002 and '03 (leading the latter race for 91 laps before cutting a tire) and winning there in '04.

TROUBLE SPOTS: Talladega has been rough for Sadler—literally: An end-over-end wreck ended his '03 race with seven laps left, and another accident in '04 sent him barrel-rolling across the finish line.

PROJECTION: He won't sneak up on anyone in '05, but with Roush muscle, the talented and reliable Sadler is a dark horse for the Cup.

FAST FACT
The 6' 2" Sadler earned a basketball scholarship to James Madison but hurt his knee.

How to explain his ascendancy? In a word, *horsepower*. In the off-season Yates and fellow Ford owner Jack Roush agreed to form an engine development partnership. (Unlike the Chevy and Dodge teams, the Ford teams to that point did not share information.) Though each owner regarded the other as a sworn enemy, they understood that an alliance would benefit both. So Roush moved his equipment and personnel into Yates's 85,000-square-foot engine shop in Mooresville, N.C. "We took parts from both our engines, and we were able to increase our horsepower," Roush says. As Sadler puts it, "The Fords actually have a gun at a gunfight now."

With all that power under his right foot, Sadler drove his M&Ms Ford to Victory Lane twice and had a career-high 14 top 10 finishes. Now one of the most reliable racers in NASCAR, Sadler is a dark horse to win it all in '05. Rest assured, his days of sneaking up on the field are over.   —L.A.

8

KaseyKAHNE

LAST SEASON: 4,274 POINTS, 13TH PLACE

THE GOLF CART WHIZZED THROUGH the garage area at California Speedway in Fontana last April 30, then slowed to pass a crush of Dale Earnhardt Jr. fans. Riding shotgun in the cart was apple-cheeked rookie Kasey Kahne. Spotting the 24-year-old racer, an Earnhardt fan with a ZZ Top beard shouted something that caused Kahne's head to turn—and his mind to spin. "Keep this up," the fan called, "and damn, Kasey, I might leave Earnhardt for you!"

Kahne flashed a smile at the fan, then NASCAR's biggest surprise of 2004 shared a secret with a passenger. "With the success I'm having," he said, "I'm seeing more and more fans starting to support me. It's unbelievable."

So was Kahne's rookie season. He won four poles, had a Series-high five second-place finishes and wound up 13th in the standings—the highest among the rookies. Though he just missed being part of the Chase for the Cup, Kahne had more top fives (13) than seven of the drivers who did qualify for the Chase, a statistic that bodes well for Kahne's 2005 title chances. "This young man has as much talent as anybody I've seen in a long, long time," says Kahne's car owner, Ray Evernham, who won three titles as Jeff Gordon's crew chief in the '90s. "When you can find someone who can

RUNS WELL AT: It's hard to spot trends after just one season, but Kahne had a hot hand in Las Vegas, where he won the pole and finished second to Matt Kenseth in just Kahne's third race.

TROUBLE SPOTS: The bumping and banging of Bristol took its toll on the rookie, whose two finishes on NASCAR's roughest track were 40th and 21st.

PROJECTION: With his 13 top five finishes, Kahne stamped himself as a contender. Look for him to win one—at least—in '05.

FAST FACT NASCAR's freshest face, Kahne signed a deal to be a spokesman for Avon products.

communicate what the car is doing while he's still learning the racetracks, as Kasey has done, they're pretty special."

Growing up in Enumclaw, Wash., Kahne started racing open-wheel cars at 14. Like other former open-wheel racers now in Nextel Cup—such as Gordon and Tony Stewart—Kahne excels at car control. His ability to keep out of trouble should make him a contender for the next decade.

"Kasey is a terrific little race car driver," says Kahne's crew chief, Tommy Baldwin. "I wouldn't trade him for any other young driver out there." —L.A.

9

kevin HARVICK

LAST SEASON: 4,228 POINTS, 14TH PLACE

KEVIN HARVICK HAS ALWAYS BEEN known for driving with feeling—sometimes too much. Yet in 2004 it was a bout of numbness that knocked the fiery driver from the Chase for the Cup. When Harvick's left arm went numb during a 229-lap green-flag run at rough-and-tumble Bristol on Aug. 28, Kyle Petty had to relieve him and Harvick ended up finishing 24th. The result left Harvick in eighth place overall, but a 28th-place finish at California Speedway a week later (Harvick was still suffering from a pinched nerve) dropped him to No. 15 and ended his 19-race stretch in the Top 10. "We had some things not go our way this year," Harvick said. "You can't expect to make those mistakes and be there."

Harvick's fall into the Nextel Cup's version of the consolation bracket was a fitting end to a curiously subdued season. The 28-year-old didn't win a race for the first time since

RUNS WELL AT: Harvick is especially Happy at Chicagoland (two victories and a top 10 in four races) and at the Indianapolis Motor Speedway (one win, average finish of 6.25).

TROUBLE SPOT: The Golden State native continues to struggle at California Speedway, with an average finish of 25.2, including the disastrous 28th that knocked him from the Chase in '04.

PROJECTION: Harvick has the hard-driving mentality to make noise in the Chase—if he can get there. We say he will, but barely.

FAST FACT
Harvick will be a car owner in the '05 Busch Series; one of his drivers will be Cup rival Tony Stewart.

taking over the late Dale Earnhardt Sr.'s ride in early 2001 and managed only five top fives and 14 top 10s after collecting 11 and 18, respectively, in '03, when he finished fifth overall. The only fireworks came on June 13 at Pocono, when Harvick traded spinouts with Matt Kenseth. Harvick got some laughs by sporting a Kenseth T-shirt under his driver's suit the next week at Michigan, but there was little cause for mirth when the man nicknamed Happy was left on the outside looking in during the final 10 races.

Even so, Harvick is a Chase contender for '05. His number 29 car failed to finish just once, when it blew an engine at Pocono on Aug. 1, ending Harvick's record of 58 straight finishes. With owner Richard Childress and crew chief Todd Berrier (with whom Harvick won the Busch title in '01), Harvick has a team built for a title run, if he can just make it to the Chase, where he may prove better suited for a furious race to the finish than he was at nursing a Top 10 position.   —*Pete McEntegart*

ryan NEWMAN

LAST SEASON: 6,180 POINTS, 7TH PLACE

THE MOST ENJOYABLE RIDE OF
Ryan Newman's 2004 season may have come as a passenger in an F-16 at Luke Air Force Base in Glendale, Ariz., last June. Newman savored the stomach-churning climbs and descents while keeping, as he put it, his "cookies in the container." Of course, Newman should be used to fast and bumpy rides. The three-year veteran has had one of the most spectacular starts in NASCAR history in terms of wins and poles, but the turbulence of accidents and engine failures has kept him from finishing in the top five in points. "It's been a roller coaster every time," Newman says. "I guess it's part of the sport when you've got 42 other competitors."

Too often it seems Newman's biggest competition is his own number 12 Alltel Dodge. The 27-year-old was a favorite for the 2004 Nextel Cup after winning a series-best eight races and 11 poles in 2003. Instead he was again bedeviled by inconsistency, with nine DNFs. He had two top fives in the last three races before the Chase to salvage the 10th and final spot, only to continue the up-and-down pattern. Newman blew an engine in the Chase's first race, at New Hampshire, to finish 33rd and put himself in a deep hole. He bounced back with a win the next week at Dover, only to follow up a 16th at Talladega by wrecking in Kansas for another 33rd, which effectively eliminated him from contention. He would grab a strong second at Phoenix, but it was too little too late as

RUNS WELL AT: Newman has won three races and collected five top 10s in six career starts at Dover's high-banked Monster Mile. He has taken three straight poles at Phoenix.

TROUBLE SPOTS: Restrictor-plate races continue to give Newman trouble, with an average finish of 21.8 and three DNFs in 12 career races at Daytona and Talladega.

PROJECTION: Newman has the talent and the team to win a title; now he needs the consistency.

FAST FACT
In 2001 Newman graduated from Purdue with a B.S. degree in vehicle structural engineering.

he finished in the seventh spot.

The brainy duo of Newman and crew chief Matt Borland, both engineers, doesn't figure to be down for long. With two wins, nine poles and 11 top fives in '04, the man who won five rookie of the year awards in various classes certainly hasn't forgotten how to run fast. If Newman and Borland can find the formula to make the dips less dramatic, the driver they call Rocketman will be poised to jet to the top.   —P.M.

jamie McMURRAY

LAST SEASON: 4,597, 11TH PLACE

NO DRIVER LAST YEAR came as tantalizingly close to NASCAR's postseason as did Jamie McMurray. In only his second full season of Cup racing, the pilot of the number 42 Dodge surged from 15th to 11th in the standings between Aug. 1 and Sept. 5, reeling off four straight top 10 finishes, but missed the Chase for the Cup by 15 points. The margin was especially frustrating for McMurray because NASCAR officials had penalized him 25 points last March after his car failed a prerace inspection at the Food City 500 at Bristol. "It's probably the most disappointing thing that's happened to me in my racing career, to come that close," McMurray says.

The penalty was a blemish on an otherwise sterling season for McMurray, 28, the 2003 Rookie of the Year. Though he finished

RUNS WELL AT: With his fifth-place finish in the Sylvania 300, McMurray notched his third top 10 at New Hampshire International Speedway in four career starts.

TROUBLE SPOT: McMurray continued to struggle at Daytona, finishing 36th in the Daytona 500 and 37th in the Pepsi 400.

PROJECTION: With another year of experience, McMurray has shown that his Rookie of the Year season was no fluke. This should be the year he gets his second win—and then some—and makes the Chase.

FAST FACT
McMurray's first win, at Lowe's in 2003, came in his second start, a modern-era NASCAR record.

the season without a win, his 23 top 10s tied for second most on the Cup circuit. Over the final 10 races he amassed the fourth-highest point total, locking up 11th place in the standings—which, as the top spot among non-Chase drivers, brought a $1 million bonus.

To place higher in '05, McMurray and crew chief Donnie Wingo must get past the engine trouble that caused McMurray to fail to finish four races last season, costing him significantly more points than any NASCAR tech inspectors. "There's not a lot you can do about it," says McMurray of his early bad luck. "This whole sport is a huge cycle. You just have to hope that it's your turn." —*Mark Beech*

mark MARTIN

LAST SEASON: 6,399 POINTS, 4TH PLACE

ON OCT. 14 MARK MARTIN announced that 2005 would be his last full season on the Cup level. The news hardly came as a shock, given that the 45-year-old driver was finishing his 21st season on NASCAR's top circuit. Indeed many observers might have expected Martin to hang up his helmet after 2003, when after finishing 13 out of the preceding 14 seasons in the Top 10 (including four runner-up spots), Martin struggled to 17th place in the standings. Yet he says he never considered retirement then.

"A lot of guys race because they love to race, but other guys race because they love to win," Martin says. "I love to win, and as long as I think I'm still able to do that, I'll keep racing."

Martin might have questioned that decision when his engine blew seven laps into the 2004 Daytona 500, relegating him to a 43rd-place finish. But new crew chief Pat Tryson brought with him a renewed optimism—along with new Ford-developed cylinder heads that gave added power to Martin's number 6 car.

The turnaround came slowly— a June win at Dover was followed

RUNS WELL AT: NASCAR's super vet is a perennial desert bloomer. In Martin's 17 career starts at Phoenix, he has finished in the top 10 on 13 occasions.

TROUBLE SPOTS: Martin has never won a Cup race at Daytona. His average finish in his 38 starts at the superspeedway is 19.5. In '04 he placed 43rd in the 500 before taking a strong sixth in the Pepsi 400.

PROJECTION: Martin has announced that '05 will be his last full Cup season. He still has the talent and the desire to make it a winning one.

FAST FACT
Martin, who is a professed fan of hip-hop, hosted MTV's *Total Request Live* in September.

by eight top fives, including a fifth at Richmond that earned him a spot in the Chase. In the hunt to the final race, Martin wound up with a popular and satisfying fourth in the standings.

Despite his impending retirement, don't expect Martin to make 2005 a mere ceremonial tour. "Respect is very important to me," he says. "I want to step out while I'm at the top of my game." —*Chris Mannix*

jeremy MAYFIELD

LAST SEASON: 6,000 POINTS, 10TH PLACE

WIN AND IN. IT'S A SPORTS cliché normally reserved for a team on the cusp of the playoffs, but it was the situation Jeremy Mayfield faced as he lined up for the Chevy Rock & Roll 400 in Richmond in September. Only a win in the final regular-season race would put Mayfield into the Chase for the Nextel Cup, a situation he had set up in the previous two weeks by finishing 22nd at Bristol and 16th at California and falling to 14th place. A year that had seen the 35-year-old Mayfield reestablish himself as a contender was turning into a disappointment.

So as Mayfield lined up for his biggest race in years, his owner and crew chief, Ray Evernham, did his best Tony Robbins impression. "Win, lose or draw, you've done a hell of a job getting us here," Evernham told his

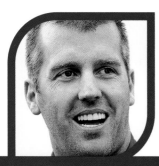

RUNS WELL AT: Mayfield has two wins and nine top 10s in 20 starts at Pocono. In '04 he finished second in the Pocono 500 in June and ninth in the Pennsylvania 500 in August.

TROUBLE SPOTS: "It's a tough place to race," Mayfield says of Martinsville. At least it is for him. His average finish at the track is 21.6, and he has just one top five finish in 19 Cup starts there.

PROJECTION: Mayfield saved his year with a win at Richmond; though snakebit in the Chase, he could well get another shot in '05.

FAST FACT
Mayfield has three Talladega poles; among active drivers only Bill Elliott (eight) has more.

driver. "We're going to go on."

Mayfield went on to lead 151 laps as he won his first race in nearly four years, a barren stretch that had humbled the driver. Although Mayfield had looked like a young lion when he ended the 1998 season seventh, by 2001 his results were so mediocre that Penske dropped him, and though Evernham signed him for '02, he soon was on the verge of losing that ride. But in '03 he signed a two-year extension, and in '04 Evernham's patience was rewarded. Though a 38th at Talladega in October ended any hopes of a title, Mayfield proved that he could be a contender. He will carry that playoff confidence into 2005.

—*Richard Deitsch*

dale JARRETT

LAST SEASON: 4,214 POINTS, 15TH PLACE

THINGS GOT UGLY FOR Dale Jarrett early last season. So ugly that some observers snickered that the driver of the number 88 UPS Ford might be more competitive against one of his sponsor's brown trucks. Well, Jarrett got the last laugh in 2004. Though he was not among the 10 drivers to qualify for the Chase for the Nextel Cup, Jarrett delivered the goods, ending the year with four top 10 finishes in the final 10 races and a respectable 15th in the standings.

It was a remarkable turnaround given that the 48-year-old driver had started 2004 the way he had ended the previous year: in a slump. The '99 champ, Jarrett finished 26th in the standings in '03, and in the first 14 races of '04 he could muster no better than a ninth place, at Atlanta. But beginning with a third at Michigan on June 20, Jarrett began to improve. Under new crew chief Mike Ford, who rejoined Robert Yates Racing last season after working with Jarrett from '95 through '00 (Jarrett had 21 victories and 104 top five finishes in that span), the team found its footing late in

RUNS WELL AT: Among active drivers only Jeff Gordon has more wins at the Brickyard than Jarrett, who has two firsts and five top fives in 11 starts at the Indianapolis Motor Speedway.

TROUBLE SPOTS: Homestead-Miami Speedway has not been kind to Jarrett. He finished fifth at the 1.5-mile oval in 1999, but his average finish since then has been 24.6, including a 24th in '04.

PROJECTION: Under crew chief Mike Ford, Jarrett showed he's still capable of top five finishes—and maybe even of a victory.

FAST FACT
Dale Jarrett Racing Adventure is the fastest-growing NASCAR driving school in the country.

the year. "We weren't even looking to get back into the top 10; this was a rebuilding year," Ford said. The strong finish puts the number 88 team ahead of schedule. Jarrett told North Carolina's *Gaston Gazette* in August that he was committed to at least two more seasons at the Nextel Cup level, and one thing is certain: No one will be using Dale Jarrett's name in a punch line anytime soon.   —R.D.

bobby**LABONTE**

LAST SEASON: 4,277 POINTS, 12TH PLACE

VERY QUIETLY BOBBY

Labonte has forged a superb career, with 21 wins and the 2000 Winston Cup title to his credit. After a 16th-place points finish in '02, he bounced back in '03 under new crew chief Michael (Fatback) McSwain to place eighth. For all their success, however, the soft-spoken Labonte and the exuberant McSwain never really bonded. "We've been pretty consistent," Labonte said last May, when he stood seventh in the standings, "but not quite as consistent as we need to be."

For Labonte, who has failed to finish a race just seven times in the past two years, consistency is everything. So it seemed strange last July when, with only nine races left before the start of the Chase, Joe Gibbs Racing released McSwain as Labonte's crew chief

RUNS WELL AT: With six Cup victories (in 24 career starts), Labonte is the reigning master of the Atlanta Motor Speedway.

TROUBLE SPOTS: Labonte's 11th-place finish at the Daytona 500 in '04 marked the 10th time in 12 starts that he has failed to make the top 10 in the season opener.

PROJECTION: Labonte went winless for the first time in 10 years in '04, but he finished the season strong. With new crew chief Steve Addington on board in '05 Labonte has reason to believe he can restart the streak.

FAST FACT
Labonte last season helped to build a quarter-midget racetrack near Salisbury, N.C.

and replaced him with Brandon Thomas, who had been part of the Gibbs engineering department. At the time Labonte stood sixth in the points, with nine top 10 finishes in 17 starts. Over the next two months his team fell apart, failing to qualify for the Chase. (He would finish the season in 12th.) "The chemistry wasn't working," said Gibbs V.P. Jimmy Makar of the decision to let McSwain go.

Whatever the explanation, the move didn't pan out, and on Dec. 1, Thomas was replaced by Steve Addington, who had worked on the Busch Series in '04. "I think he'll be able to help us get back to Victory Lane and into the championship hunt," Labonte said.   —*Mark Beech*

---

brian**VICKERS**

LAST SEASON: 3,521 POINTS, 25TH PLACE

THERE MAY COME A TIME

when Brian Vickers looks back fondly on his Nextel Cup rookie season. But give him a few years.

Vickers went from the top of the Busch Series standings in 2003 to the middle of the Nextel Cup pack in '04, a year that included more wrecks than wins. The rookie's hit list included Bobby Labonte (Pocono), Ryan Newman (Indianapolis) and Dale Jarrett (Watkins Glen). At Sonoma he tangled with Tony Stewart, and the two exchanged words after the race, an incident that ended with Stewart striking Vickers with an open palm. (NASCAR fined Stewart $50,000.) "Some were just racing incidents, and some were solely my fault," says Vickers, 21. "What happened at Watkins Glen with Dale was a case of me being way too impatient at that point in the race. It's been a learning year."

There were highlights, too, including Vickers's becoming the youngest pole sitter in NASCAR history, at the Chevy American Revolution 400 in Richmond last May. He also had ninth-place finishes at Michigan and

RUNS WELL AT: Vickers set a qualifying record at Richmond, where track position means everything, and finished eighth, his best finish of 2004. As a Busch Series driver, he had wins at Dover and Darlington.

TROUBLE SPOTS: Vickers says he loves superspeedway racing, but he has yet to find success at Talladega, where he finished 27th in the spring race and 36th last fall.

PROJECTION: Hendrick Motorsports has invested plenty in Vickers, and the talent is there. A win or two is a reasonable goal.

FAST FACT
Early in the 2002 season Vickers missed his high school prom because he was racing at Bristol.

Daytona and ended '04 in 25th place, 12 spots behind Rookie of the Year Kasey Kahne. "A lot of things were the same in the Busch Series, but there is just so much more of it at the Nextel Cup level," Vickers says. "The schedule and competition are more intense. Responsibilities from sponsors and the media are more intense. It's tough. But that's what the rookie season is for—to learn and grow."   —R.D.

carl EDWARDS

LAST SEASON: 1,424 POINTS, 37TH PLACE

THE MOST SIGNIFICANT

event to occur in the aftermath of Carl Edwards's season-opening Craftsman Truck Series win at Daytona wasn't the backflip the 25-year-old did off the bed of his truck in Victory Lane. Rather, it was a comment his team owner, Jack Roush, made in the postrace press conference, "Carl Edwards is the heir apparent to Mark Martin in the number 6 car." It seemed a fitting cap to Edwards's rags-to-riches story: Before Roush called him in 2003 and offered him a one-year ride in the truck series, Edwards, who was taking classes at Missouri and working as a substitute teacher, was considering giving up racing and joining the military. He jumped at Roush's offer and finished eighth as a truck rookie.

But, like most of the vehicles he drives, Edwards's rise through the

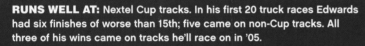

RUNS WELL AT: Nextel Cup tracks. In his first 20 truck races Edwards had six finishes of worse than 15th; five came on non-Cup tracks. All three of his wins came on tracks he'll race on in '05.

TROUBLE SPOTS: Fridays. As solid as Edwards was on race day in his 13 Nextel Cup outings, he was mediocre at best in qualifying, earning a top 15 starting spot only three times.

PROJECTION: Edwards is a talented driver who's racing for a top team. There's no reason he can't hover around the top 10.

FAST FACT
Edwards came up with his signature backflip as a tribute to his idol Ozzie Smith.

NASCAR ranks kept accelerating. In August, Jeff Burton left Roush's Nextel Cup team, and Edwards was installed in the 99. Though he had to juggle his new duties with a full truck schedule, Edwards fared well in both. He was fourth in the truck standings, and in his first 13 Cup starts he had five top 10s—two more than Burton had in 22 races in the same car. With the luxury of being able to focus on one series, Edwards could give Roush the kind of results he saw the last time he took a kid (Matt Kenseth) under his wing. "I want to get the growing pains out of the way," Edwards said late in the '04 season, "so we can race for the championship next year."
—*Mark Bechtel*

jeff BURTON

LAST SEASON: 3,902 POINTS, 18TH PLACE

THE RECRUITMENT BEGAN

several years ago as the late Dale Earnhardt Sr. was beginning to contemplate retirement. Earnhardt would see Jeff Burton in the garage or he'd wander over to Burton's motor home, and he would put the hard sell on the young driver the Intimidator hoped would one day take his seat in the legendary number 3 car at Richard Childress Racing.

"Dale was wearing me out," Burton, 37, recalled in 2004. "He was pretty big on me going over there and driving. I had my commitments and loyalty to Roush Racing."

Though Earnhardt wasn't around to see it, Burton finally did leave Roush Racing and move to Richard Childress Racing midway through last season. Burton didn't make it to Victory Lane after switching from Roush's number 99 Ford to Childress's number 30 Chevrolet on Aug. 22, but he did show signs of resuscitating his flagging career. In 14 races with Childress, Burton recorded 10 top 15 finishes and at times showed the flash of the Burton of old, the gutsy driver who

RUNS WELL AT: Burton has always been known as a formidable restrictor-plate racer, and in '04 he produced two solid runs at Talladega, finishing seventh in the spring and 13th in the fall.

TROUBLE SPOTS: The Pocono triangle was trying for Burton in '04. He finished 24th at the Pocono 500 in June and 34th seven weeks later at the Pennsylvania 500.

PROJECTION: Burton should rebound in '05, but don't look for the driver of the late '90s—who was in the Top 10 for five straight years.

FAST FACT
An active Republican, Burton hopes one day to run for a seat in the U.S. Senate.

between 1997 and 2000 won 15 Cup races. (In his 22 races with Roush in 2004, Burton had just nine top 15 finishes and looked like he was on the road to unemployment.) "Jeff's a championship-caliber driver," says new boss Childress. "This thing ain't going to turn around overnight. But by being able to start out this year with us, it's going to give him a huge advantage for 2005."
—*L.A.*

greg BIFFLE

LAST SEASON: 3,902 POINTS, 17TH PLACE

UNTIL GREG BIFFLE TOOK the checkered flag in the GFS Marketplace 400 at Michigan International Speedway in August, his 2004 season had been a major disappointment. A rookie star two years ago, the 35-year-old driver had only one top 10 finish in his first 19 races and had spent most of the year outside the Nextel Cup Top 20. "Anybody that was happy with that performance," Biffle says, "needs to quit racing."

Biffle was mad enough to consider leaving the five-car Roush Racing operation, which included three drivers who would make the Chase: Kurt Busch, Matt Kenseth and Mark Martin. For all Biffle's potential, he was hardly the star of the team, and there was speculation that his status kept him from getting the best equipment. "I was real close

RUNS WELL AT: After struggling with the tight turns at Pocono in '03, Biffle put together two good runs at the track last year, finishing 11th and fourth in his two trips to Pennsylvania.

TROUBLE SPOTS: No track was tougher on Biffle last year than the California Speedway, where he finished 33rd and 36th.

PROJECTION: The team assembled by Biffle and crew chief Doug Richert endured growing pains last year but closed with a win. Riding that momentum, Riggs can expect to visit Victory Lane again in '05.

FAST FACT
Biffle got started in the sport by street racing in his hometown of Vancouver, Wash., when he was 17.

[to leaving]," he said. "We didn't have the best race cars at times." That changed over the second half of the season, as owner Jack Roush affirmed his support for Biffle and crew chief Doug Richert. Though still plagued by inconsistency, Biffle had seven top 10s over the final 17 races, including wins at Michigan in August and at Homestead in the season finale.

That victory, the third of Biffle's Cup career, was a tremendous confidence booster—and a hint that the only driver in NASCAR history to have won championships in both the Craftsman Truck Series (2000) and the Busch Series (2002) may yet have a shot at the title trifecta.　—*Mark Beech*

scott RIGGS

LAST SEASON: 3,090 POINTS, 29TH PLACE

RUSSELL RIGGS IS NOT an unreasonable man. When he decided that racing motorcycles was getting too dangerous for his 16-year-old son Scott, he didn't force him to take up chess or origami. No, after selling Scott's motocross bikes one day while he was at school, Russell told his son any racing he did in the future would be on four wheels.

That decision put Scott on a slow road to Nextel Cup racing. Now 34, he just missed out on the young-gun era, when a kid could get a shot without being proven. So he worked his way up through the ranks—"I feel like I may be one of the last people to come through the good, old-fashioned way," he says—conquering Mini Stocks, Late Models, trucks and the Busch Series, where he was atop the standings heading into the final race in 2003 before an early-lap wreck ended his title hopes. That got Riggs a seat with MBV Motorsports, a Cup team in transition. Pontiac pulled out of the sport, forcing the team to get used to Chevrolets, and Riggs struggled in the new setup.

"We had a lot of things going against us to start off," team

RUNS WELL AT: Talladega. He qualified well at the superspeedway (fifth and fourth) and showed he was learning the draft. After a 34th-place finish in his first Talladega race, he was 11th in his second.

TROUBLE SPOTS: Fifty-eight drivers tried to make the October Atlanta race, and Riggs, who finished 25th at the track in March, was one of the 15 who failed—the only time he missed a race.

PROJECTION: A year under his belt and a knack for avoiding trouble (he completed 90.8% of his laps in '04) give Riggs a shot at the Top 20.

FAST FACT
Last June, Riggs entered his first ARCA event, to get experience at Pocono—and won the race.

V.P. Jim Rocco said last summer. "But we're starting to make progress. This year is really getting ready for 2005." By the end of the season Riggs had shown enough promise (in his final seven races he started in the top 10 three times and had three top 15 finishes) to warrant Rocco's optimism for the '05 season—and to make his father's decision to sell his bikes seem pretty wise.　—*Mark Bechtel*

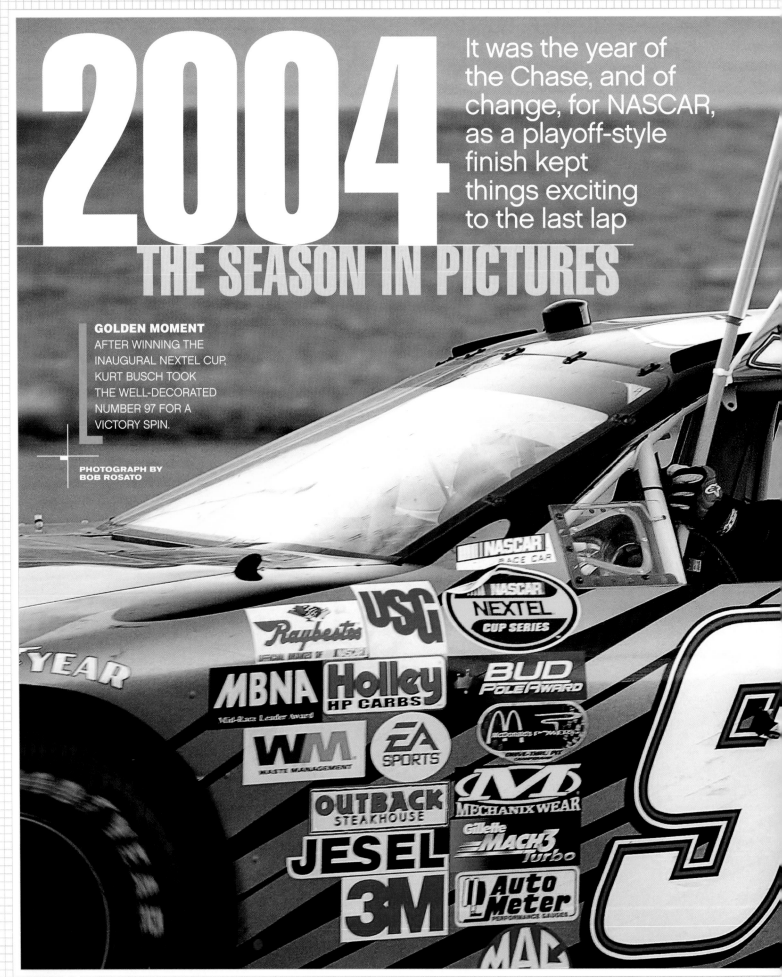

2004
THE SEASON IN PICTURES

It was the year of the Chase, and of change, for NASCAR, as a playoff-style finish kept things exciting to the last lap

GOLDEN MOMENT
AFTER WINNING THE INAUGURAL NEXTEL CUP, KURT BUSCH TOOK THE WELL-DECORATED NUMBER 97 FOR A VICTORY SPIN.

PHOTOGRAPH BY
BOB ROSATO

2.15

DAYTONA 500

DAYTONA INTERNATIONAL
SPEEDWAY

WINNER: DALE EARNHARDT JR.

Junior was feeling bubbly after
winning, in only his fifth season, the
race it took his father 20 tries to
conquer. "I know Dad was over
in the passenger side with me," he
said. "I'm sure he was having a
wonderful time."

**PHOTOGRAPH BY JEFF SINER/
CHARLOTTE OBSERVER/ABACA**

2.22

SUBWAY 400

NORTH CAROLINA
SPEEDWAY

WINNER: MATT KENSETH

It was the most exciting race
of the 2004 season: Kenseth
(17) nosed out rookie Kasey
Kahne by .01 of a second to
win one of the closest races
in NASCAR history. If only
they could all end this way.

**PHOTOGRAPH BY JUSTIN
HINSHAW/CHARLOTTE
OBSERVER/ABACA**

3.7

**UAW-DAIMLER
CHRYSLER 400**

LAS VEGAS
MOTOR SPEEDWAY

WINNER: MATT KENSETH

Kenseth's second straight
victory—of the year and at
Las Vegas—vaulted the
2003 points champion right
back to the top of the
Nextel Cup standings.

**PHOTOGRAPH BY
NIGEL KINRADE**

3.14

GOLDEN CORRAL 500

ATLANTA MOTOR SPEEDWAY

WINNER: DALE EARNHARDT JR

A day after Junior served as
best man for a Florida couple
who were married in a Victory
Lane ceremony, his number 8
Chevrolet blew away the
competition at Atlanta and he
won the 11th race of his career
by more than four seconds.

**PHOTOGRAPH BY
KARIM SHAMSI-BASHA**

A new scoring format helped NASCAR shake things up as the Nextel era made a spirited debut at the Daytona 500

Compiled by Trisha Blackmar

SIMPLY splashing

3.21

CAROLINA DODGE DEALERS 400

DARLINGTON RACEWAY

WINNER: JIMMIE JOHNSON

Johnson (48) crossed the starting line just ahead of Bobby Labonte. They would finish the same way almost 300 laps later, with Johnson taking the checkered flag by .132 of a second.

PHOTOGRAPH BY DONALD MIRALLE/GETTY IMAGES

3.28

FOOD CITY 500

BRISTOL MOTOR SPEEDWAY

WINNER: KURT BUSCH

Although he ignored orders from crew chief Jimmy Fennig to come in for fresh tires with 119 laps to go and fought a poor-handling car all day, Busch still won his third straight race at Bristol.

PHOTOGRAPH BY CHRIS STANFORD/ GETTY IMAGES

4.4

SAMSUNG/ RADIO SHACK 500

TEXAS MOTOR SPEEDWAY

WINNER: ELLIOTT SADLER

While Kasey Kahne again played the bridesmaid— finishing second for the third time in seven races—Sadler scored the win in the second-closest finish of the season.

PHOTOGRAPH BY WORTH CANOY/ICON SMI

RACE 8

4.18

**ADVANCE
AUTO PARTS 500**

MARTINSVILLE SPEEDWAY

WINNER: RUSTY WALLACE

Evidence of a so-called "dogfight"
was all over Wallace's number 2
Dodge as the 47-year-old traded
plenty of paint en route to his 55th
win. He blew by Jimmie Johnson
(48) with 45 laps left and then
battled Bobby Labonte to the finish.

PHOTOGRAPH BY DON KELLY

RACE 9

4.25

AARON'S 499

TALLADEGA SUPERSPEEDWAY

WINNER: JEFF GORDON

Fans threw bottles and other
garbage onto the track to protest
NASCAR's decision to keep
Gordon (left) in the lead even
though he appeared to have been
passed by Dale Earnhardt Jr.
before the final caution.

PHOTOGRAPH BY
PHIL CAVALI/ASP INC.

RACE 10

5.2

AUTO CLUB 500

CALIFORNIA SPEEDWAY

WINNER: JEFF GORDON

Gordon (here being
congratulated by crew chief
Robbie Loomis on his 66th
career win) pitted for fuel with
52 laps to go and finished an
astonishing 12.87 seconds
ahead of the field.

PHOTOGRAPH BY
CIA STOCK PHOTO

RACE 11

5.15

**CHEVY AMERICAN
REVOLUTION 400**

RICHMOND INTERNATIONAL
RACEWAY

WINNER: DALE EARNHARDT

Strategy proved more important
than speed for Junior (8), who
chose to stay on the track instead
of pitting for fresh tires with
45 laps remaining. The decision
paid off with a win.

PHOTOGRAPH BY
SAM SHARPE

5.30
COCA-COLA 600
LOWE'S MOTOR SPEEDWAY

WINNER: JIMMIE JOHNSON

After getting a boost from SpongeBob, Johnson was cartoonishly dominant at Charlotte, getting his second '04 win, leading 334 of 400 laps and holding a 20-car lead at one point in the race.

PHOTOGRAPH BY PHIL CAVALI/ASP INC.

6.6
MBNA 400
DOVER INTERNATIONAL SPEEDWAY

WINNER: MARK MARTIN

Martin (6) barely avoided doing the Monster mash and held on to take the checkered flag for the first time in 72 races. "Everything worked out in our favor, but believe me, we were due," Martin said.

PHOTOGRAPH BY DAVID VAUGHN/WIREIMAGE.COM

RACE 14

6.13
POCONO 500
POCONO RACEWAY

WINNER: JIMMIE JOHNSON

It was no reach to say that Johnson had one of the strongest cars all year. "I have 100 percent confidence in my car, my team, my abilities," he said after leading 126 of 200 laps at Pocono. "That allows us to bounce back even if we have a bad week."

**PHOTOGRAPH BY
CIA STOCK PHOTO**

RACE 15

6.20
DHL 400
MICHIGAN INTERNATIONAL SPEEDWAY

WINNER: RYAN NEWMAN

Despite losing a lap early in the race because his car was overheating, Newman (12) was one "lucky dog." A caution on Lap 175 allowed him to rejoin the lead pack and go all the way to the checkered flag.

**PHOTOGRAPH BY
CHRIS STANFORD/GETTY IMAGES**

RACE 16

6.27
DODGE/ SAVE MART 350
INFINEON RACEWAY

WINNER: JEFF GORDON

Gordon's record eighth road-course win required some creative thinking: To conserve fuel over the last 42 laps he had to resort to shutting off his engine while rolling downhill under caution.

**PHOTOGRAPH BY
CIA STOCK PHOTO**

RACE 17

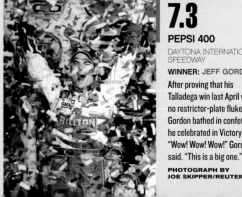

7.3
PEPSI 400
DAYTONA INTERNATIONAL SPEEDWAY

WINNER: JEFF GORDON

After proving that his Talladega win last April was no restrictor-plate fluke, Gordon bathed in confetti as he celebrated in Victory Lane. "Wow! Wow! Wow!" Gordon said. "This is a big one."

**PHOTOGRAPH BY
JOE SKIPPER/REUTERS**

RACE 18   RACE 19   RACE 20

7.11

TROPICANA 400

CHICAGOLAND SPEEDWAY

WINNER: TONY STEWART

A messy postrace wrestling match erupted in the pits as a result of eventual winner Tony Stewart (Home Depot team) having bumped then leader Kasey Kahne on Lap 127, sending Kahne spinning.

PHOTOGRAPH BY ROBERT SUMNER/ JOLIET HERALD NEWS

7.25

SIEMENS 300

NEW HAMPSHIRE INTERNATIONAL SPEEDWAY

WINNER: KURT BUSCH

"I believe our chase for the championship started today," a confident Busch said after his dominating win at Loudon moved him from ninth to sixth in the points standings.

PHOTOGRAPH BY WORTH CANOY/ICON SMI

8.1

PENNSYLVANIA 500

POCONO RACEWAY

WINNER: JIMMIE JOHNSON

JJ's number 48 Chevy was just a blur to the rest of the field as he became the first driver since Bobby Labonte in 1999 to sweep both races at Pocono in a single season. It was his fourth win of the year.

PHOTOGRAPH BY JONATHAN FERREY/ GETTY IMAGES

8.8
BRICKYARD 400
INDIANAPOLIS MOTOR SPEEDWAY

WINNER: JEFF GORDON

Gordon and the rest of his crew earned the right to kiss the bricks at Indy after he became NASCAR's first four-time winner at the famed track, equaling the totals of past Indy 500 champions A.J. Foyt, Al Unser Sr. and Rick Mears.

PHOTOGRAPH BY DARRELL INGHAM/GETTY IMAGES

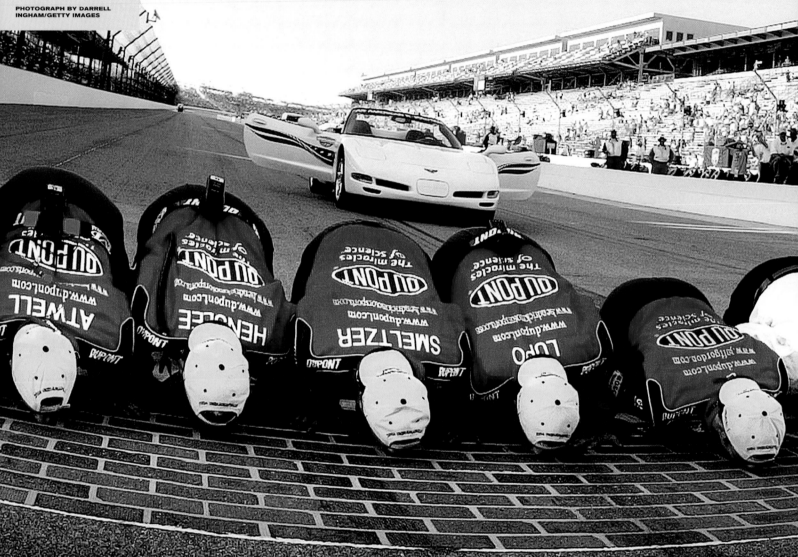

8.15
SIRIUS AT THE GLEN
WATKINS GLEN INTERNATIONAL SPEEDWAY

WINNER: TONY STEWART

Stomach cramps plagued Stewart during the race, but they couldn't slow him down for long. "With a car like we had today, I wasn't going to take a win away from [my team]," he said.

PHOTOGRAPH BY PHIL CAVALI/ASP INC.

8.22
GFS MARKETPLACE 400
MICHIGAN INTERNATIONAL SPEEDWAY

WINNER: GREG BIFFLE

With a car he described as being "pretty danged fast," Biffle (in front) led 73 laps and pulled away from teammate Mark Martin after taking four tires on his final pit stop for the second win of his career.

PHOTOGRAPH BY LEON HALIP/WIREIMAGE.COM

8.28
SHARPIE 500
BRISTOL MOTOR SPEEDWAY

WINNER: DALE EARNHARDT JR.

A day after winning the Busch race, Junior lapped more than half the field in the Sharpie 500. The win, which was the 13th of his career, put Earnhardt third in the points and gave him some much-needed momentum heading into the Chase for the Championship.

PHOTOGRAPH BY SAM SHARPE

RACE 25

9.5

POP SECRET 500

CALIFORNIA SPEEDWAY

WINNER: ELLIOTT SADLER

Sadler's surprising season continued in Fontana, where his number 38 Ford pulled away from Mark Martin and Kasey Kahne on a restart with 10 laps to go and clinched a berth in the Chase.

**PHOTOGRAPH BY
CIA STOCK PHOTO**

RACE 26

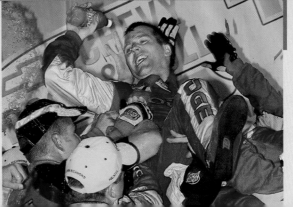

9.11

CHEVY ROCK AND ROLL 400

RICHMOND INTERNATIONAL SPEEDWAY

WINNER: JEREMY MAYFIELD

It was mayhem for Mayfield (top) in Victory Lane after the 35-year-old driver raced his way into the Chase field with this win at Richmond.

**PHOTOGRAPH BY
MATT THACKER/ASP INC.**

THE CHASE SO FAR . . .
A win in the Chase opener vaulted Busch from seventh into a tie for the points lead, while Newman (33rd) and Mayfield (35th) dug early holes.

RANK, DRIVER	+/- RANK CHANGE	CUP POINTS
1 Dale EARNHARDT JR.	+2	5,210
2 Kurt BUSCH	+5	5,210
3 Jeff GORDON	–2	5,201
4 Matt KENSETH	+1	5,200
5 Jimmie JOHNSON	–3	5,180
6 Elliott SADLER	—	5,172
7 Mark MARTIN	+1	5,139
8 Tony STEWART	–4	5,086
9 Ryan NEWMAN	+1	5,074
10 Jeremy MAYFIELD	–1	5,068

RACE 27

9.19
SYLVANIA 300
NEW HAMPSHIRE INTERNATIONAL SPEEDWAY
WINNER: KURT BUSCH
A week after he ran out of gas while leading at Richmond with eight laps left, Busch (Irwin) was fully fueled in New Hampshire, leading 155 of the 300 laps on the way to his second Loudon victory of the 2004 season.

PHOTOGRAPH BY MICHAEL J. LEBRECHT II

NEXTEL CUP 2004
THE CHASE FOR THE CUP

THE chase IS ON

NASCAR's first playoff season produced down-to-the-wire drama and a rock-steady new champion

Compiled by Richard O'Brien

9.26

MBNA AMERICA 400

DOVER INTERNATIONAL
SPEEDWAY
WINNER: RYAN NEWMAN

Newman mashed Dover's
daunting Monster Mile—as well
as the rest of the field—in
streaking to his second victory of
the season. Eight of the top 10
spots in the race were taken by
drivers in the Chase.

**PHOTOGRAPH BY
CHRIS STANFORD/GETTY IMAGES**

THE CHASE SO FAR . . .

Four-time champ Gordon took third
to regain the points lead, while
Martin's strong second put him in the
hunt; '03 champ Kenseth wrecked.

RANK, DRIVER	+/– RANK CHANGE	CUP POINTS
1 Jeff GORDON	+2	5,371
2 Kurt BUSCH	—	5,370
3 Dale EARNHARDT JR.	–2	5,353
4 Jimmie JOHNSON	+1	5,314
5 Mark MARTIN	+2	5,314
6 Elliott SADLER	—	5,275
7 Matt KENSETH	–3	5,272
8 Ryan NEWMAN	+1	5,264
9 Tony STEWART	–1	5,236
10 Jeremy MAYFIELD	—	5,214

RACE 29

10.3

EA SPORTS 500

TALLADEGA
SUPERSPEEDWAY
WINNER: DALE EARNHARDT JR.

It may not have meant, um, diddly
to Earnhardt, but his dramatic,
come-from-behind win gave him
five victories at Talladega, a total
second only to the 10 scored by
another plainspoken fella by the
name of Earnhardt.

**PHOTOGRAPH BY
SAM SHARPE**

THE CHASE SO FAR . . .
Another top 10 kept Busch atop the standings, while Sadler's fourth-place finish (best among the Chasers) put him in the mix.

RANK, DRIVER		+/- RANK CHANGE	CUP POINTS
1	Kurt Busch	—	5,685
2	Dale EARNHARDT JR.	—	5,656
3	Jeff GORDON	—	5,606
4	Elliott SADLER	+4	5,542
5	Mark MARTIN	+1	5,535
6	Tony STEWART	—	5,512
7	Matt KENSETH	-2	5,505
8	Ryan NEWMAN	-1	5,453
9	Jimmie JOHNSON	—	5,438
10	Jeremy MAYFIELD	—	5,428

10.10
BANQUET 400
KANSAS SPEEDWAY
WINNER: JOE NEMECHEK

They call him Front Row Joe, and Nemechek lived up to his nickname, taking the pole and, here, edging Ricky Rudd at the finish line. The victory reminded everyone that there was still life outside the Chase.

PHOTOGRAPH BY JIM BARCUS/ KANSAS CITY STAR/ KRT/ABACA

10.16
UAW-GM QUALITY 500

LOWE'S MOTOR
SPEEDWAY
WINNER: JIMMIE JOHNSON

For most of the final night race of
'04 the spotlight was on rookie
Kasey Kahne, who led 207 laps
before a blown tire sent him into
the wall, allowing Johnson to grab
the victory over teammate Gordon
(who survived a wreck of his own).

**PHOTOGRAPH BY
JIM GUND**

THE CHASE SO FAR . . .

Johnson won the race—on his home
track—but gained only a spot as
Busch, Junior, Gordon, Sadler and
Stewart all finished in the top 10.

RANK, DRIVER		+/- RANK CHANGE	CUP POINTS
1	Kurt BUSCH	—	5,850
2	Dale EARNHARDT JR.	—	5,826
3	Jeff GORDON	—	5,776
4	Elliott SADLER	—	5,693
5	Mark MARTIN	—	5,664
6	Tony STEWART	—	5,646
7	Matt KENSETH	—	5,635
8	Jimmie JOHNSON	+1	5,623
9	Ryan NEWMAN	−1	5,579
10	Jeremy MAYFIELD	—	5,501

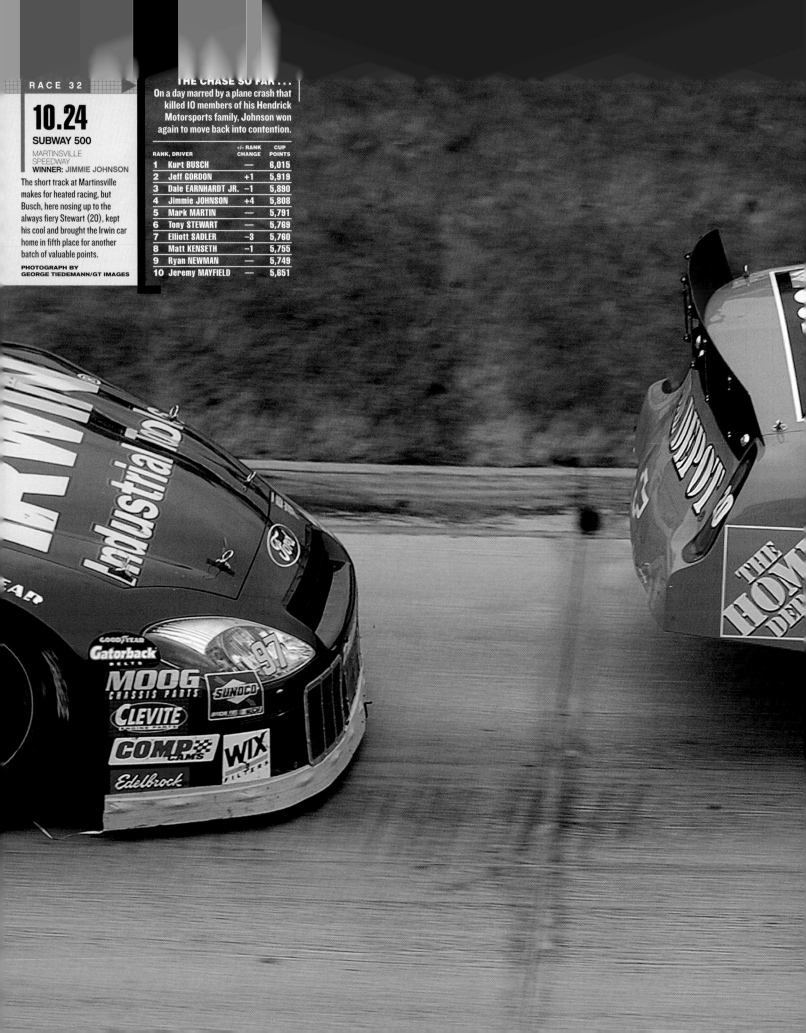

10.24

SUBWAY 500

MARTINSVILLE
SPEEDWAY
WINNER: JIMMIE JOHNSON

The short track at Martinsville makes for heated racing, but Busch, here nosing up to the always fiery Stewart (20), kept his cool and brought the Irwin car home in fifth place for another batch of valuable points.

PHOTOGRAPH BY
GEORGE TIEDEMANN/GT IMAGES

THE CHASE SO FAR . . .

On a day marred by a plane crash that killed 10 members of his Hendrick Motorsports family, Johnson won again to move back into contention.

RANK, DRIVER		+/- RANK CHANGE	CUP POINTS
1	Kurt BUSCH	—	6,015
2	Jeff GORDON	+1	5,919
3	Dale EARNHARDT JR.	−1	5,890
4	Jimmie JOHNSON	+4	5,808
5	Mark MARTIN	—	5,791
6	Tony STEWART	—	5,769
7	Elliott SADLER	−3	5,760
8	Matt KENSETH	−1	5,755
9	Ryan NEWMAN	—	5,749
10	Jeremy MAYFIELD	—	5,651

RACE 33

10.31

BASS PRO SHOPS MBNA 500

ATLANTA MOTOR SPEEDWAY
WINNER: JIMMIE JOHNSON

Hats turned backward in memory of Ricky Hendrick, their team owner's son who was lost in the previous week's plane crash, Johnson (left) and Gordon celebrated Johnson's victory.

PHOTOGRAPH BY
WALTER ARCE/ASP INC.

THE CHASE SO FAR . . .

Busch's first Chase letdown—a blown engine—left him 42nd, while Johnson won yet again; a late-race accident cost Junior a shot at victory.

RANK, DRIVER	+/- RANK CHANGE	CUP POINTS
1 Kurt BUSCH	—	6,052
2 Jimmie JOHNSON	+2	5,993
3 Jeff GORDON	−1	5,980
4 Mark MARTIN	+1	5,971
5 Dale EARNHARDT JR.	−2	5,954
6 Tony STEWART	—	5,907
7 Ryan NEWMAN	+2	5,866
8 Elliott SADLER	−1	5,815
9 Matt KENSETH	−1	5,795
10 Jeremy MAYFIELD	—	5,736

THE CHASE SO FAR . . .
Junior's win vaulted him to third,
leaving the top four within 48 points
with two races to go; Newman's
strong second was too little, too late.

RANK, DRIVER	+/- RANK CHANGE	CUP POINTS
1 Kurt BUSCH	—	6,191
2 Jeff GORDON	+1	6,150
3 Dale EARNHARDT JR.	+2	6,144
4 Jimmie JOHNSON	−2	6,143
5 Mark MARTIN	−1	6,089
6 Tony STEWART	—	6,049
7 Ryan NEWMAN	—	6,041
8 Elliott SADLER	—	5,869
9 Matt KENSETH	—	5,855
10 Jeremy MAYFIELD	—	5,836

THE CHASE SO FAR . . .
Dominating on the way to his fourth Chase victory, Johnson closed in on the still-steady Busch (who took sixth) as Earnhardt (11th) lost ground.

RANK, DRIVER	+/- RANK CHANGE	CUP POINTS
1 Kurt BUSCH	—	6,346
2 Jimmie JOHNSON	+2	6,328
3 Jeff GORDON	−1	6,325
4 Dale EARNHARDT JR.	−1	6,274
5 Mark MARTIN	—	6,264
6 Tony STEWART	—	6,161
7 Ryan NEWMAN	—	6,102
8 Matt KENSETH	+1	5,963
9 Elliott SADLER	−1	5,963
10 Jeremy MAYFIELD	—	5,942

RACE 35

11.14

SOUTHERN 500

DARLINGTON RACEWAY
WINNER: JIMMIE JOHNSON

Hardly lying down on the job, the Sharpie crew hammered out a rubbing fender during a Lap 120 pit stop. Restarting in 25th place, Busch climbed back into the top 10 and, thanks to another sharp stop with 36 to go, finished sixth.

PHOTOGRAPH BY JIM GUND

THE CHASE CONCLUDES . . .
Johnson and Gordon gave it their all, finishing second and third, respectively, but Busch, dodging disaster, took fifth—and the Cup.

RANK, DRIVER		+/- RANK CHANGE	CUP POINTS
1	Kurt BUSCH	—	6,506
2	Jimmie JOHNSON	—	6,498
3	Jeff GORDON	—	6,490
4	Mark MARTIN	+1	6,399
5	Dale EARNHARDT JR.	-1	6,368
6	Tony STEWART	—	6,326
7	Ryan NEWMAN	—	6,180
8	Matt KENSETH	—	6,069
9	Elliott SADLER	—	6,024
10	Jeremy MAYFIELD	—	6,000

RACE 36

11.21
FORD 400
HOMESTEAD-MIAMI SPEEDWAY
WINNER: GREG BIFFLE

On a banner day for NASCAR and Nextel, Biffle (16)—here leading, from left, Roush Racing teammate Busch, Gordon and Kevin Harvick—held off Johnson and Gordon in a last-lap dash to help secure the title for Busch.

**PHOTOGRAPH BY
BILL FRAKES**

The heart
of NASCAR
beats on in the
roar of distant
races and in
the voices of
its pioneers

LIVING
legends

LET'S GO RACIN'
ON JUNE 19, 1960, NASCAR SPED INTO CHARLOTTE WITH THE FIRST WORLD 600 (WON BY JOE LEE JOHNSON).

PHOTOGRAPH BY DON HUNTER

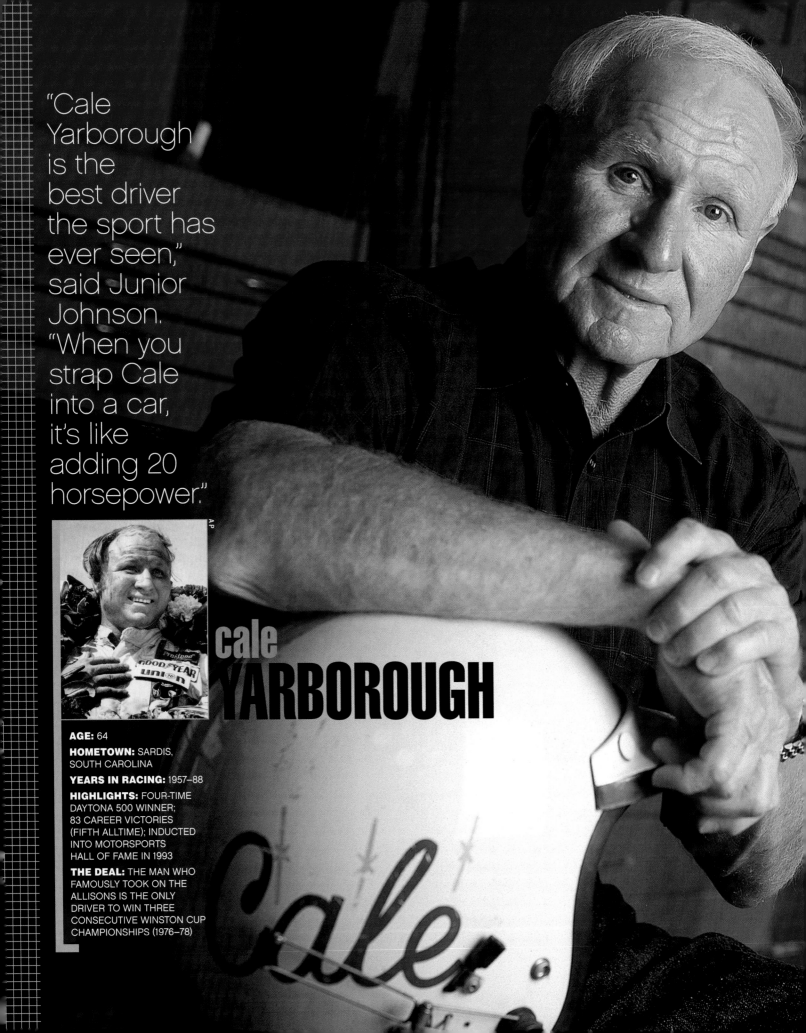

"Cale Yarborough is the best driver the sport has ever seen," said Junior Johnson. "When you strap Cale into a car, it's like adding 20 horsepower."

cale YARBOROUGH

AGE: 64

HOMETOWN: SARDIS, SOUTH CAROLINA

YEARS IN RACING: 1957–88

HIGHLIGHTS: FOUR-TIME DAYTONA 500 WINNER; 83 CAREER VICTORIES (FIFTH ALLTIME); INDUCTED INTO MOTORSPORTS HALL OF FAME IN 1993

THE DEAL: THE MAN WHO FAMOUSLY TOOK ON THE ALLISONS IS THE ONLY DRIVER TO WIN THREE CONSECUTIVE WINSTON CUP CHAMPIONSHIPS (1976–78)

titans
OF THE TRACK

For these NASCAR immortals, whose talents helped make the sport a modern-day colossus, the passion still runs deep

PHOTOGRAPHS BY GREG FOSTER
TEXT BY RICHARD DEITSCH

CALL IT THE ULTIMATE NASCAR FANTASY CAMP.
Last August photographer Greg Foster chewed tobacco with Cale Yarborough, talked engine-building with Cotton Owens, and stuck close to Junior Johnson's bumper as the racing legend puttered around Wilkes County in North Carolina. As part of an assignment to photograph some of the living legends of NASCAR (whose portraits fill these pages), Foster traveled more than 3,500 miles throughout North and South Carolina, a 15-day odyssey up and down Interstate 85. He got the idea for the project around Christmas 2003 while he and his wife, Jennifer, were en route to Martinsville, Va., to visit relatives. "It was real quiet in the car, and I just imagined all these NASCAR guys who lived on either side of I-85," says Foster, whose work has also appeared in FORTUNE, MONEY and TIME. "I wanted to chronicle history passing. Like the picture with Cotton Owens *[page 103]*. The engine on the lift was one of the hemi engines he had in 1964. The next year they outlawed the engine because it was so powerful."

Foster, who grew up in Griffin, Ga., five miles from Atlanta Motor Speedway, has long been a fan of racing's iconic figures. "I don't think any of them think of themselves as legends," Foster says. "They're probably aware of it, but they're pretty humble people—basically, just a bunch of good ol' guys."

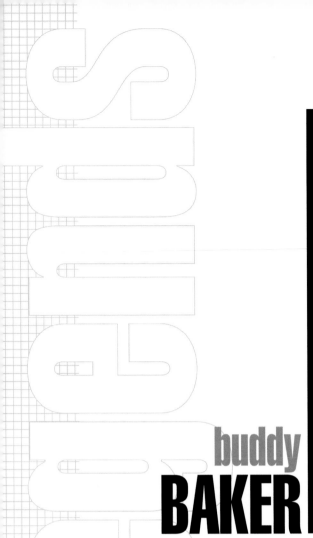

legends

AGE: 64

HOMETOWN: LAKE NORMAN, NORTH CAROLINA

YEARS IN RACING: 1959–92

HIGHLIGHTS: FOUR-TIME WINNER AT TALLADEGA AND CHARLOTTE; 19 CAREER WINS; INDUCTED INTO MOTORSPORTS HALL OF FAME IN '97

THE DEAL: THE SON OF NASCAR LEGEND BUCK BAKER WAS THE FIRST DRIVER TO WIN RACING'S BIG FOUR: CHARLOTTE (1967), DARLINGTON ('70), TALLADEGA ('75) AND DAYTONA ('80)

AP

buddy
BAKER

"The cars practically drive themselves these days," said Baker. "If I had known the cars would be this easy to drive, I wouldn't never had retired."

"I've never driven on a racetrack as fast as I've driven on the road," said Johnson. "But of course, when I quit racing [in 1966], we were only running about 180 down the backstretch at Daytona."

MIKE STALEY COLLECTION

junior
JOHNSON

AGE: 73

HOMETOWN: HAMPTONVILLE, NORTH CAROLINA

YEARS IN RACING: 1953–95

HIGHLIGHTS: WON 50 WINSTON CUP RACES, INCLUDING 1960 DAYTONA 500; CAR OWNER FOR CURTIS TURNER AND DARRELL WALTRIP, AMONG OTHERS

THE DEAL: JOHNSON WAS THE SUBJECT OF TOM WOLFE'S SEMINAL 1965 *ESQUIRE* MAGAZINE PIECE, "THE LAST AMERICAN HERO IS JUNIOR JOHNSON. YES!"

AGE: 80

HOMETOWN: SPARTANBURG, SOUTH CAROLINA

YEARS IN RACING: 1946–81

HIGHLIGHTS: NINE WINS ON WINSTON CUP CIRCUIT; WON MORE THAN 100 MODIFIED RACES IN THE 1950s; VOTED ONE OF NASCAR'S 50 GREATEST DRIVERS IN 1998

THE DEAL: AFTER HIS DRIVING CAREER, OWENS BECAME A CAR OWNER FOR BUDDY BAKER, RALPH EARNHARDT AND DAVID PEARSON, AMONG OTHERS

DOZIER MOBLEY

cotton
OWENS

"We didn't have seat belts, so we had to tie ourselves in the car with a rope," said Owens of his first Southern 500, in 1950. "And the doors had handles, so we had to tie them shut with a dog collar."

"I was just born to be wild," said Smith. "I tried to be a nurse, a pilot and a beautician and couldn't make it in any of them. But from the moment I hit the racetrack, it was exactly what I wanted."

louise
SMITH

AGE: 88

HOMETOWN: GREENVILLE, SOUTH CAROLINA

YEARS IN RACING: 1946–56

HIGHLIGHTS: FIRST WOMAN TO RACE AT NASCAR'S TOP LEVEL; WON 38 RACES AT LOCAL SHORT TRACKS RACING IN MIDGETS, MODIFIEDS, SPORTSMAN AND LATE MODEL CARS

THE DEAL: IN 1999 THE PIONEERING SMITH BECAME THE FIRST WOMAN INDUCTED INTO THE MOTORSPORTS HALL OF FAME

AGE: 70

HOMETOWN: SPARTANBURG, SOUTH CAROLINA

YEARS IN RACING: 1960–86

HIGHLIGHTS: GRAND NATIONAL TITLES IN '66, '68 AND '69; 105 WINS, SECOND ALLTIME TO RICHARD PETTY; PEARSON AND PETTY FINISHED ONE-TWO 63 TIMES (PEARSON WON 33 OF THOSE RACES)

THE DEAL: PEARSON'S WINNING PERCENTAGE OF 18.29% IS BEST ALLTIME AMONG DRIVERS COMPETING IN AT LEAST 240 RACES

LANE STEWART

david PEARSON

"He's the best there's ever been," said Cotton Owens of Pearson. "He could do good in any kind of car. He just knew how to make cars go, and he was so smart he could beat people that way."

NASCAR legends
RICHARD PETTY

PHOTOGRAPH BY GREG FOSTER

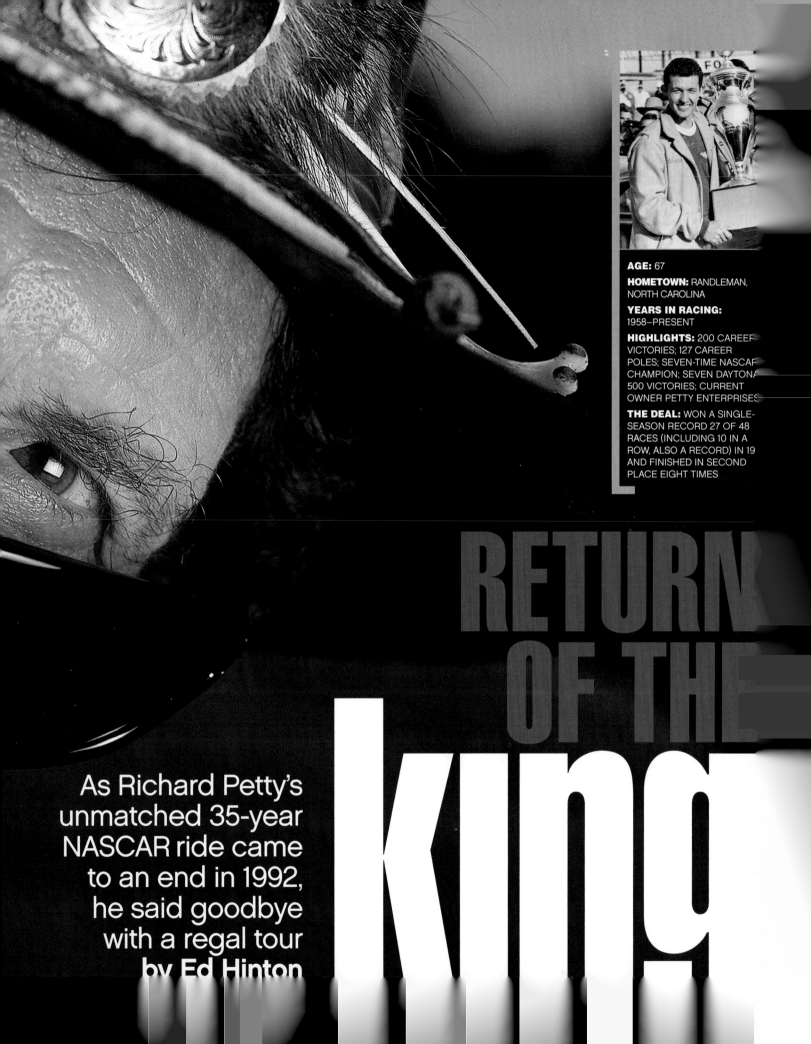

AGE: 67

HOMETOWN: RANDLEMAN, NORTH CAROLINA

YEARS IN RACING: 1958–PRESENT

HIGHLIGHTS: 200 CAREER VICTORIES; 127 CAREER POLES; SEVEN-TIME NASCAR CHAMPION; SEVEN DAYTONA 500 VICTORIES; CURRENT OWNER PETTY ENTERPRISES

THE DEAL: WON A SINGLE-SEASON RECORD 27 OF 48 RACES (INCLUDING 10 IN A ROW, ALSO A RECORD) IN 19 AND FINISHED IN SECOND PLACE EIGHT TIMES

RETURN OF THE king

As Richard Petty's unmatched 35-year NASCAR ride came to an end in 1992, he said goodbye with a regal tour
by Ed Hinton

DOWN THE FINAL STRETCH, IN THE WANING WEEKS OF HIS CAREER, RICHARD PETTY

can hardly hear the crowds roaring their farewells. He is 55 years old and partly deaf. The engines have sung to him for too long—through 35 years and 200 major stock car racing wins and passage into blue-collar legend. • After the Oct. 11, 1992, Mello Yello 500 in Charlotte, only three races remain

in this, Petty's final season of driving. Three more races, and there will be rest for the lanky frame that has been battered literally from head to foot—from concussions to broken toes, with all kinds of damage in between. In 1980 Petty drove with a broken neck, knowing that even a bump from another car could kill him. But the most telling setback occurred in '78, when 40% of his ulcer-ravaged stomach was surgically removed, likely the price of being too nice to too many people for too long.

"Sometimes," he says, "it's a blessing to be hard of hearing."

Petty has given every bit of himself to the sport he personally brought out of the backwoods and off the bootlegger trails. He is NASCAR's Arnold Palmer. When motor racing fans speak of the King, they don't mean Elvis.

"There are no more Richard Pettys here," says his son, Kyle, 32, himself a 14-year veteran NASCAR driver. "Nobody to pick up where he'll leave off. And that is going to be a major problem for the sport. It's not so much what he's won. Forget winning 200 races, seven championships, seven Daytona 500s [all records]. I'm talking about the Richard Petty who sits on a pit wall and signs autographs for four hours."

FIRST FAMILY LEE, CENTER, WAS THE FOUNDER OF THE EMPIRE THAT INCLUDED SONS MAURICE (LEFT) AND RICHARD.

You can't compare a man doin' it for money with a man doin' it for love. Richard done it when there weren't no money."

[pioneer NASCAR driver Lee Petty] taught me was, Don't get above your upbringing," he says.

When Richard, sprung from a hamlet with the salt-of-the-earth name of Level Cross, N.C., says "I knowed," it is not out of ignorance but rather folksiness, the way Woody Guthrie sang, "I been havin' some hard travelin'/I thought you knowed."

"What helps with people," says Petty, "is when, even though you've won a lot of money and been to see several presidents—you know, done the things they would like to do—they can still talk to you on their terms. I talk football with them, religion with them, or I can talk about the kids back there in the swimming hole. It don't make any difference."

The final deluge of emotion for the King will come in Atlanta on the weekend of Nov. 14. The night before the last race of the season, Petty will appear before 75,000 of his closest followers in the new Georgia Dome, with the country-music group Alabama singing goodbye.

But Petty's most significant parting has already taken place. He has raced his last at Daytona International Speedway. The man and the track made each other famous. His

Petty has named his final rounds as a driver his Fan Appreciation Tour. Few figures in American sports have appreciated their fans as much as Petty has; few, if any, have reciprocated as thoroughly by mingling with the crowd. Petty does not tower over his followers so much as minister to them. He is of them and among them. One by one, hour by hour, day by day since 1958, he has not only shaken their hands and signed their photos, but he has also talked to them—"talked to me just like I was somebody," as so many have said so often.

He talks to them in their vernacular. For the sake of his fans, he has cultivated the image of a good ol' boy, one he could have shaken decades ago had he wanted to. He says, "I can't talk good English," but in fact he chooses not to. "One of the first lessons my daddy

seven victories in the Daytona 500 are as many as the second- and third-best achievers have managed together. The man and the event are synonymous; no one has ever gained so much attention for losing a race as Petty did at the 500 in 1976, when he and David Pearson crashed into each other with the checkered flag in sight.

He hasn't won on the NASCAR circuit since 1984, admitting that "the legend part is what has kept Richard Petty going." But that final victory provided just the sort of material that seals legends: It was Petty's 200th, and it came at his beloved Daytona, not in the 500 but in the Firecracker 400, on the Fourth of July, with President Ronald Reagan looking on.

For the fans the memories—and Petty's diligent acknowledgment of his faithful's adoration—are enough to keep him the King, despite eight years of not winning. For his farewell tour he has allowed himself a sanctuary, a luxury motor coach in which to rest at each track, because the fans and the media have multiplied so greatly.

HANDS-ON PETTY, WHO DIDN'T HESITATE TO WORK ON HIS OWN CAR, MADE A DELICATE ADJUSTMENT AT A DAYTONA RACE.

"The greatest luxury of this bus is the bathroom," he says, emerging from the toilet. "I can go whenever I like. Out in the garage area it takes half an hour to get from my race car to the rest room [through mobs of autograph seekers] and half an hour to get back." He could have hidden in a motor coach for the past 20 years, as drivers often do nowadays. But Petty remained among the people—smiling, signing, always smiling, always signing—one-hour trips to the bathroom and all.

He and his family have paid a price for his success and popularity. In 1967 Petty won 27 races (out of 48), a record that will be virtually impossible to break because NASCAR's Winston Cup tour now counts only 29 races. After that grinding '67 season, says Lynda, Petty's wife of 33 years, "we had plans to go to Panama to visit some friends. But at the last minute Chrysler Corporation needed him to do something [Plymouths wore Petty's number 43 in those days; Pontiacs have since 1982]. I ended up flying with three children down to Miami and then to Panama, all of us really upset that he didn't get to go. Since then I don't know how many times he has come to me and said, 'I hate to tell you this, but. . . .' And I would take the children and go on. We've learned to live that way."

Even the Pettys' avocations are public. Back home in North Carolina, Richard serves on the Randolph County Commission—salary $200 a month—and Lynda sits on the county school board. "He's never been a hunter or a fisherman or a golfer," says Lynda. "He does have a tractor with a bush hog. He's cut roads all through these woods [their 500-acre spread in Level Cross]. He gets on his four-wheeler and rides those roads for hours, and nobody bothers him. That's the nearest thing to a hobby he has."

He will not even suggest that the weight of being the King may have had something to do with his ulcer surgery of '78. At the time, he says, "I wasn't eating right, wasn't sleeping right, wasn't doing anything right, and it all caught up with me. A lot of it could have been mental. I don't know. I can't separate those things."

That was the year his slip from the pinnacle began. He suffered through the first big losing streak of his career, going winless through all of '78. While other NASCAR teams went high-tech, refining aerodynamics and chassis with more-sophisticated engineering and less hard-knocks savvy, Petty Enterprises remained complacent. "We'd been winning for 20 years and decided we wouldn't change," Petty says. "We should have led the way [in technology], but we didn't even follow." And so his dominance ebbed, but not the legend.

In fact his image may have helped to hasten his downfall, for he was simply too busy with the public to spend time with his mechanics improving the team's race cars.

In 1986 Petty gave some telling advice to the young Bill Elliott, who was hurtling into stardom and baffled by the limelight. "You've got to grin and bear it while you're there," Petty told him. "Then you can go out behind the building to cuss and throw up."

Any NASCAR star will sign autographs nowadays—for $10,000 per session or on orders from a corporate sponsor. And the young guns sometimes hand out machine-printed autographs. But, says Petty, "everything that's supposed to be autographed, I sign." For 35 years he has signed his name, on average, 600 times a day. He signs in his office in the morning, on private and commercial planes, at public appearances, at home at night, right up until bedtime; he signs posters, souvenirs, letters, trading cards, toys. He personally signs every response to every letter in the full mailbag that arrives every day at his racing compound in Level Cross. He long ago mastered a handwriting technique that utilizes the muscles in his arm rather than his hand, so he won't get writer's cramp.

Big Jesse Sykes, who at 450 pounds is an unofficial Petty bodyguard and something of a sage in the garages, stuffs his catcher's-mitt hands into his overalls and remarks on the drivers of past and present. "You can't compare a man doin' it for money with a man that done it for love," he says. "Richard done it when there weren't no money."

In the years when NASCAR was just emerging from the dirt tracks, "we didn't have sponsors," says Petty. "We didn't have nobody to please. We didn't have nobody to tell us when to do right. We just done it. To begin with, it was an honor—still is. But a cat from Level Cross, never been nowhere, he goes down to South Carolina or up to New York and somebody wants his autograph. It was a big deal. Big honor. Once you got doing it, you didn't mind doing it. You seen how it pleased the people. It just happened. The good Lord just does these things, and I don't know why, and the people don't know why."

"Nobody fills those shoes," says driver Darrell Waltrip, who seemed to think that *he* could when he exploded onto the NASCAR scene in the 1970s, young, articulate, brash and talented. Waltrip at first thought NASCAR needed a new, more polished hero—a Waltrip—to purge the sport of the good-ol'-boy stereotypes of

IN DEMAND THOUGH HIS DAD MISSED MANY FAMILY TRIPS, KYLE (RIGHT, AGE 11) GOT CLOSE TO HIM AT THE TRACK.

For the sake of his fans, he has cultivated the image of a good 'ol boy, one he could have shaken had he wanted to.

FRONT-RUNNER PETTY REMAINS THE WINNINGEST DRIVER AT DAYTONA (10), THOUGH HE FINISHED 26TH HERE IN 1977.

Petty's generation. With avalanches of boos, the public let Waltrip know it liked the King and his realm just fine. And for years, every time the aggressive Waltrip so much as rubbed fenders with another driver, his roller-coaster image would take a plunge. Waltrip, now 45 and wiser, says, "The thing that has impressed me most through the years about Richard is his image. Through the good times and the bad times, that has never changed."

Petty has been involved in fender-banging feuds, most notably a running war with Bobby Allison in the early '70s. But he has never had the bad-guy label hung on him.

"Richard was made for this sport, or this sport was made for Richard—however you want to look at it," says Waltrip. "It was as if Richard had written the script and NASCAR just helped him play it out. And anybody else who tried to come in, tried to get a leading role, had to be the bad guy."

For almost 20 years Pearson was the perennial other guy, though not so much the bad guy as simply not Petty. "I was bashful," says Pearson. "I'd hide from the media, and Richard would talk to them. I once saw him ask a TV reporter if he wanted an interview. I'd never have done such a thing. It hurt me in the long run. Richard did it the right way."

Aficionados will say that Pearson was a better driver than Petty—smoother and wilier. Says Petty, "Pearson could beat you on a short track, he could beat you on a superspeedway, he could beat you on a road course, he could beat you on a dirt track. It didn't hurt as bad to lose to Pearson as it did to lose to some of the others, because I knew how good he was."

"We finished one-two more than anybody else ever did," Pearson says. The Petty-Pearson quinella came in a remarkable 63 times between 1963 and '77, with Pearson holding a 33–30 edge. But of all those races, one stands out most keenly in Petty's mind. It was the 1976 Daytona 500. On the final lap the two came flying side by side through the high-banked third turn, Pearson completing a classic "slingshot" pass. But Petty counterpunched, regaining the lead through the fourth and final turn with an unprecedented sort of re-slingshot. As they entered the homestretch, Petty pinched Pearson into the outside retaining wall. Pearson collided with Petty but was able to keep his engine running. Petty, his car fishtailing

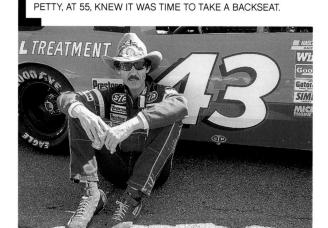

QUITTIN' TIME AFTER FOUR DECADES BEHIND THE WHEEL, PETTY, AT 55, KNEW IT WAS TIME TO TAKE A BACKSEAT.

etty has given every bit of himself to the sport. When motor racing fans speak of the King, they don't mean Elvis.

from the impact with Pearson's, continued several hundred yards before hitting the wall. As Petty's Dodge sat smoking, immobile, Pearson drove his wrecked Mercury under the checkered flag at 10 mph to win the 500.

Of all the drivers from other forms of racing who came to run occasionally in NASCAR—from Jim Clark to Mario Andretti—A.J. Foyt is the one Petty would have loved to face on a regular basis. "If Foyt had run with us full time," Petty says, "nobody might have ever heard of Richard Petty." He grins. "Then again, nobody might have ever heard of A.J. Foyt."

Above all, Foyt sensed a bedrock toughness in Petty. Foyt, the raging bull, has always worn his toughness on his sleeve. Petty has worn his in his hip pocket, seldom visible but always ready. In 1971 and '72 he and Allison engaged in their notorious feud, knocking each other's cars all over virtually every NASCAR track in America. Finally they held peace talks. "As far as I'm concerned, it's over," Petty told Allison, then a wiry welterweight of a man. "But if I hear one more word you've said in the media, I'm gonna beat the livin' ---- out of you."

Allison, the same age as Petty and a friend since the feud ended, was not able to choose the time of his retirement. A near-fatal brain injury, suffered in a crash at Pocono Raceway in 1988, made his decision for him. He has since recovered enough to lead a fairly normal life but not to race. "I guess I pity more than envy" Petty's having to make a decision to retire, Allison says. "He's earned the right to run until he's 90 if he wants to."

Foyt announced in 1991 that the Indy 500 that year would be his last, then changed his mind. He couldn't bring himself to quit. Petty says his decision is final. "He won't come back," says Kyle. "It's been too hard to get to this point to have to go through it again."

Petty will remain around racing as a car owner. "Even though he's a legend and he's done more for the sport than anyone could even sit down and think about, he'll still be just an owner," says Kyle, "not Richard Petty getting his 200th win or Richard Petty making his 1,500th start. Just an owner. He has to deal with that. He'll still be nice to people, but the Richard Petty y'all know will be dead. He'll be standing there in the pits, but you'll know he'd give everything he had, all 200 wins, all seven championships, if he could go just one more time. Guys like Daddy and A.J., guys who have done this for so long, they look at quitting as terminal illness. They look at this year as the last few days of their lives." ▫

OPPOSITE, CLOCKWISE FROM TOP LEFT: PRYOR/AP; MIKE ADASKAVEG/STOCK CAR RACING MAGAZINE; AP; GEORGE TIEDEMANN/GT IMAGES

LUCKY ROLL THOUGH HIS NUMBER 43 ROLLED SEVEN TIMES, PETTY EMERGED UNHURT FROM THIS '88 DAYTONA WRECK.

AGES: BOBBY (LEFT, TOP AND INSET), 67; DONNIE, 65

HOMETOWNS: LAKE NORMAN, N.C.; SALISBURY, N.C.

YEARS IN RACING: 1961–88; 1966–88 (DRIVING)

HIGHLIGHTS: COMBINED FOR 94 WINS (BOBBY HAD 84, DONNIE HAD 10); BOBBY IS NOW VP OF ARNOLD MOTORSPORTS; DONNIE WORKS AS A CONSULTANT TO NASCAR DRIVERS

THE DEAL: BOBBY, DONNIE AND SPORTSMAN DIVISION LEGEND RED FARMER FORMED THE BARNSTORMING ALABAMA GANG IN THE '50S.

sur

His sons are gone, his body is battered, but Bobby Allison

PHOTOGRAPH BY GREG FOSTER

COMPETITION PROVEN
UNION 76
Holley
CARBS

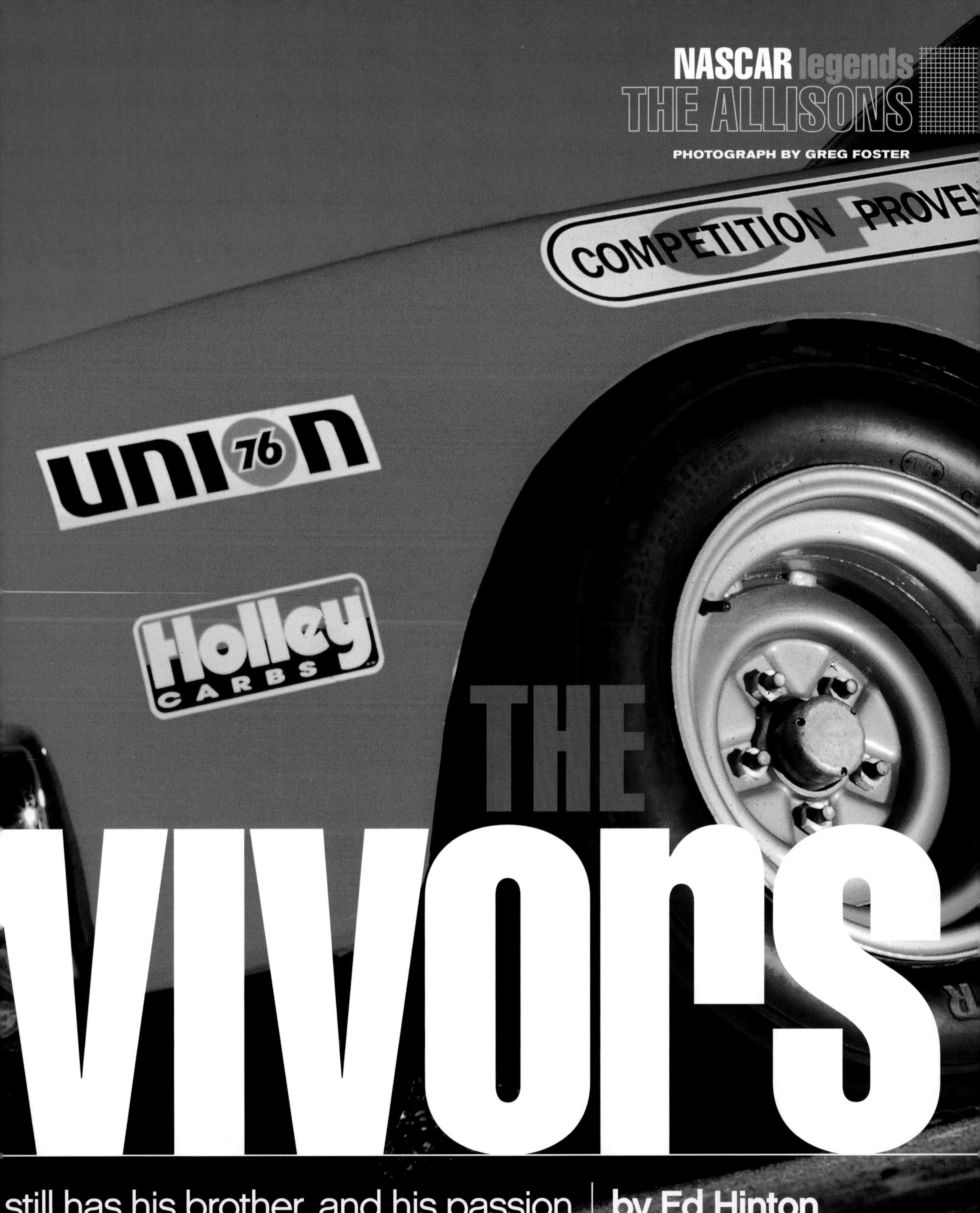

THE vivors

still has his brother, and his passion | **by Ed Hinton**

THE FOR SALE SIGN LIES BLOWN DOWN IN THE YARD AT 135 CHURCH AVENUE IN

Hueytown, Ala., and the big ranch-style house looks forlorn. Inside it is even grimmer. The house was emptied at auction last March. Who knows when it might sell, haunted as it is by all that sorrow. • "We moved in on Christmas Eve, 1969," says Bobby Allison. "Worst day of the year to move. But I thought it

would be neat for those kids to wake up in that new house and find that Santa Claus had been there."

Allison now lives across the street in a modular home. He is back with his mother, Kitty, after 40 years as maybe the most independent-minded man on earth. On the dead lawns between the two houses there is silence, save for the wind blowing leaves through what's left of Bobby's life.

He is 59, and Kitty is 90. "This is Bobby Allison. Is my mommy over there?" he sometimes asks neighbors on the phone in a mock-childlike tone, cheerfully acknowledging the irony of his living arrangement. Kitty is back to waiting up for him at night and picking up his ice-cream bowls. Everybody else is as gone as the millions of dollars that have passed through his hands.

Down the hill from the big house are two sprawling, empty buildings—Bobby's former racing shops, where his two sons apprenticed to his perilous trade. Beyond the buildings lies the fishpond where Bobby's family and friends used to take short breaks from the long hours of work and cast for bass.

Time was when the melancholy aftermath of Christmas would give way to a happy February in the Allison compound, as the family made its bustling departure for Daytona Beach and the bright beginning of a new NASCAR season. This year Bobby will limp out of his house alone and head southeast to hail the resumption of a sport that has left him behind—broke and almost broken, but not brooding. Allison does not brood. He goes on.

For the first time since he started in the sport, Allison goes to Daytona as an outsider. The North Carolina–based racing team he partly owns has fallen apart, sponsorless and driverless. He goes on.

Bobby and his wife of 36 years, Judy, separated a year ago. Their divorce proceedings, which batter the spirit of this profoundly Catholic man, won't be settled until May at the earliest. He goes on.

"Some . . . incidents . . . in my life kept the agony, kept the agony, kept the agony on her," Bobby says. Not by accident does he say the phrase three times: Once for his near death and the handicaps he still suffers. Once for the death of Clifford, his loving and mischievous son,

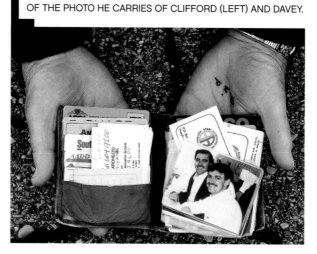

KEEPSAKE "THIS TELLS THE WHOLE STORY," SAYS BOBBY OF THE PHOTO HE CARRIES OF CLIFFORD (LEFT) AND DAVEY.

Says Bobby, his voice dwindling to a whisper as he recalls the day Clifford died, "His last words to me were, 'We're gonna get 'em, Dad.' "

the one Bobby most cherished. Once for the death of Davey, the determined, self-sufficient, sometimes defiant son, the great success, the one most like his father. "So she packed her suitcase, and she left," Bobby continues. "I felt the agony too. But I handled it differently. I've always had this . . . this . . . ability to . . . go on."

Their sons died pursuing passions that he gave them: driving race cars and flying aircraft. "I still don't know whether I blame myself about Clifford," Bobby says. "But racing took Clifford. And racing was my . . . my . . . whole life.

"Racing didn't take Davey. Judy was really bitter about the helicopter. She said racing bought it for him. I said Davey would have mowed grass to buy that helicopter. Judy said racing bought Davey the helicopter. I think one of the things that happened to Judy and me was that we were not able to give each other the support we should have in this incredible tragedy." Even before the formal separation, Bobby continues, "we would go in separate directions a lot. She would go stay with her sisters. A friend of mine had a house in Pensacola, and I would get in my plane and go stay with him, and we'd get on his boat. Somehow I could hide."

Judy, who lives in an apartment in nearby Hoover, Ala., says she isn't bitter toward racing. "And I didn't really leave," she adds, measuring her words in light of the ongoing divorce proceedings. She will not discuss the reasons for the separation except to say, "I do not feel it was the deaths of the boys." Of Allison family life and its attendant tragedies, she says only, "I think this whole situation has been oversimplified [by the media]. It would take a whole year's issues of SPORTS ILLUSTRATED to get all of this the way it should be."

"This has been going on, and off, for about 25 years," says the Allisons' eldest daughter, Bonnie, 34, of her parents' marital strain. "But through it all, Dad and Mom were so strong in their faith that divorce was out of the question until Davey and Clifford died."

A searching look troubles Bobby's face as he tries to make things

HARD MILES ALLISON IS TIED FOR THIRD ALLTIME WITH 84 CAREER VICTORIES, BUT HE IS NASCAR'S LEADER IN HEARTACHE.

add up in a mind that is hazy in some places and totally dark in others, where certain precious memories should be. This is the result of brain damage he suffered in a crash at Pocono (Pa.) Raceway on June 19, 1988. "Life-threatening" inadequately describes the accident, which was sickening to behold. Death had Bobby Allison in that wreckage on the backstretch, had him firmly, until a paramedic climbed into the car and performed the tracheotomy that gave him a thread to hang by.

Davey Allison would later recall how that night, after emergency neurosurgery was performed on his father, "the doctor called me over into a corner. He said, 'Son, tonight you're going to have to make yourself be the man of this family. Because if your daddy lives through the night, he'll probably never be able to do anything again.' It took the breath out of me. It took my legs out from under me. I fell straight down onto the floor."

But somewhere deep in his coma, Bobby's enormous will took charge. He fought off death, fought through unconsciousness, rose and walked. But, says Judy, "Bobby went all the way back to being a baby. He had to be retaught everything: going to the bathroom, brushing his teeth, taking a bath, getting dressed, everything. Who do you think did that [with him]?" Gradually Bobby recovered the majority of his mind. This last miracle he accomplished during the eight agonizing months between the crash and the day he limped triumphantly onto the track at Daytona in February 1989. Clifford and Davey were both competing in that year's Speed Weeks. "I . . . am . . . very . . . glad," Bobby said then with terrible difficulty, "that . . . both . . . Davey . . . and Clifford . . . are . . . out there . . . racing . . . because . . . there is . . . a lot . . . more good . . . out there . . . than . . . bad."

"I meant that," Bobby says now. "I still believe that."

As he slowly recovered physically, other things got worse. And worse. And worse. First he realized that he would never race in NASCAR again. Then two insurance policies failed to protect him, and he had to pay $160,000 of his medical bills himself, mainly by selling machinery he had bought after the crash to help build racing engines, because, he says, "at least that was something I could still do." (A rehab center in Birmingham let him work off a debt of about $60,000 by making public appearances and speeches.)

"I have been hurting," Allison says, "for 8½ years." He waves a hand as though it were nothing, this physical pain. "I'm hurting right now, sitting here, talking to you." His face goes somber. "But

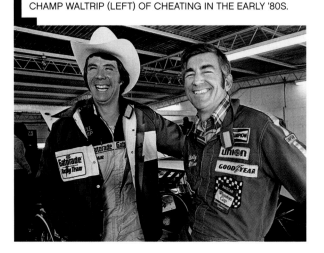

FEUDIN' ALLISON REPEATEDLY ACCUSED THREE-TIME CHAMP WALTRIP (LEFT) OF CHEATING IN THE EARLY '80S.

"One of Bobby's downfalls was that he was paranoid," says Waltrip. "No matter how well he did, he thought everybody was against him."

when I walked up to that car, as close as from me to you, and saw that boy was dead—knew that boy was dead"—his voice begins to dwindle—"there began a pain that I had never known before, never imagined. And it kept hurting. Kept hurting. Kept hurting. . . ." And has never gone away, the echo of his whisper says. Clifford still stares at him from that wreckage at Michigan International Speedway on Aug. 13, 1992. "He had a wound on his face that never even bled—that's how fast his heart stopped," Bobby says. Clifford was 27.

"If I get killed in a race car," Davey Allison once said, his brown eyes blazing with certainty, "I'm gonna die with a smile on my face." Davey died with no expression on his face, in a coma, in a Birmingham hospital on July 13, 1993, just hours after his helicopter crashed into an infield parking lot at Talladega (Ala.) Superspeedway. He and Charles (Red) Farmer, a veteran racer and longtime family friend, were flying into Talladega to watch the race car test session of David Bonnett, son of Neil Bonnett, another close family friend and an original member of the storied Alabama Gang of drivers Bobby had once led.

It was Neil who scrambled into the helicopter wreckage to rescue Farmer (who suffered fractured ribs and a broken collarbone), then went back in for Davey, who was unconscious. Seven months later Neil would die of injuries suffered in a crash during practice at Daytona. He was an ever-cheerful sort who could lighten any burden. In 1990 he had suffered a brain injury of his own in a crash. "I went over to Bobby's house to get some advice," he said later. "Between Bobby trying to think of what he wanted to say and me trying to remember what he'd just said, we had a helluva time." When Neil died, it was "another hard hit," says Bobby. "But by that point I had two things I had been through, to build my strength."

The 32-year-old Davey, like his father, was an excellent pilot of fixed-wing aircraft. But the jet helicopter was a new toy he had bought with money he earned as he hurtled toward the pinnacle of NASCAR. The helicopter was highly sophisticated, treacherous to a novice. After it crashed, the National Transportation Safety Board investigation concluded there had been pilot error.

Through it all, Bobby goes on. Occasionally he slurs a word, like someone who has had a few drinks. He walks slowly, arrhythmically, deliberately. Every step is unimaginably hard. But Bobby's injured brain and shattered left leg have healed vastly beyond his doctors'—maybe even his priest's—expectations.

Hail Mary, full of grace, the Lord is with thee. . . . You might wonder how many hundreds of thousands of Hail Marys have been said for Allison. And by him. And you might wonder why he has never uttered Ernest Hemingway's prayer of the desperate: *Hail nothing, full of nothing, nothing is with thee.*

Father Dale Grubba, a priest from Princeton, Wis., who has been a friend of the Allison family for nearly 25 years, is writing a book comparing Bobby with the Biblical figure Job. "The difference," says Father Grubba, "is that Job never had a head injury, with all the frustration, the confusion, the self-doubt that come with it. God left Job his clarity, so that he could reason through his trials."

In the end God restored Job's wealth. Allison drives a '77 Mazda pickup between his mother's house and the hangar at the Bessemer, Ala., airport where he keeps his weathered twin-engine 1981 Aerostar. (Some neurosurgeons said there was no way Allison could rehabilitate himself enough to regain his pilot's license with full instrument ratings, but he did so in 1993.) He still owns a condominium at Charlotte Motor Speedway, but it is of little use to him now that his racing team, which was based nearby, is on the verge of collapse. He still has his two daughters—Bonnie and 29-year-old Carrie—but, Carrie says, "I don't think it's possible for us to replace anything about Clifford and Davey: their time or anything else they shared with Dad."

"We've tried," says Bonnie. "We've been there, gone to races with him, but it's just different."

Carrie works as a marketing representative for Bobby Allison Motorsports, although the team survives in name only, with no driver, no sponsor and no plans to enter a car at Daytona this year. "I think Dad enjoyed having Carrie travel with the team," says Bonnie, "but that team wasn't working together."

Carrie could see that the team was causing her father more pain than joy. "I think he felt he really wasn't needed there," she says.

The disintegration of Bobby Allison Motorsports "might just be the best thing that has happened to me since 1988," Bobby says. He is tired of being a figurehead car owner, dependent on the financial backing of his partners. It isn't just that he can't drive anymore. He can't attract adequate sponsorship—even with his highly recognized name—in NASCAR's boom time, when most other teams are engorged with funding. He can't even bring himself to give orders in the pits.

He is tired of writing himself little notes of reprimand. "S---. I should have spoken up," he wrote into his worn little notebook in October 1996, moments after his driver, Derrike Cope, had been

FIGHTIN' BOBBY (LEFT) TUSSLED WITH YARBOROUGH AT DAYTONA IN '79 IN ONE OF NASCAR'S DEFINING MOMENTS.

I knew what was going to happen," says Donnie of his brother's fight with Yarborough. "I'd seen that look on Bobby's face before."

caught up in a crash at Rockingham, N.C., destroying one of the few good vehicles the Allison team had left. There went another $100,000. Just before the crash Allison had reckoned the car should be called into the pits for some adjustments. Others on the crew didn't see the need Allison saw, and he kept quiet. "If I'd said something, taken charge, ordered Derrike in, he wouldn't have been out there where the wreck started," Allison says. "But that old thing keeps biting at me. Lack of confidence." Since his own accident and recovery he simply hasn't trusted his own thoughts.

"A lot of people have tried to help him get his confidence back," says Carrie, "and there have been some who, though they haven't meant to, have contributed to his lack of confidence. If he made a suggestion, they'd either ignore him or laugh. They made him feel like he didn't know what to do or say."

Bobby Allison was a cornerstone of NASCAR's formative years, from the late '60s to the late '80s. "Yesterday," he says, with all the emptiness a man can put into one word.

But being a living legend paid well for Allison, at least until October, when his towering pride reared its head and he cut off his own paycheck. He had a contract with the Alabama Department of Transportation to do television spots, personal appearances and lectures on safe driving in exchange for up to $75,000 a year. But, he says, "I got criticized." He had been recruited by Governor Fob James, a Republican. Then Allison met, and liked, Jeff Sessions, a Republican candidate for the U.S. Senate. They took some bus tours around the state together, making speeches. Then Alabama newspaper columnists assailed the Republicans and Allison for perceived logrolling—"saying that I had made all this money, and now I was ripping off the state of Alabama," Allison says. On Oct. 23, on another bus tour, Allison picked his spot. He gathered two Birmingham TV crews and announced that he would continue to do the safety appearances, but at no charge. "So far, I think I've earned $48,000," Allison said into the microphones. "The contract called for up to $75,000 a year, for two years."

"So you're giving up more than $100,000?" a reporter asked.

"Whatever it is," Allison said, and he shrugged. The cameras stayed on him. "I can take care of my personal bills." (He makes a little money from public appearances for corporations and from the use of his name by a chain of cellphone stores.) "I have been in a financial pinch for 90 percent of my adult life. I'm pretty fortunate that people like [90-year-old] Mrs. Shepherd, who lives up there at the beginning of Church Avenue in Hueytown, will feed me if I show up hungry."

The interview was aired on Birmingham newscasts that night. Allison had the last word, the cost be damned.

"Sounds just like him," says Richard Petty, his grin rife with 30 years of memories of his once bitter rival. "Same old Bobby, saying, 'O.K., boys, you wanna play? I'll play with you. But we're gonna play by my rules.'"

"It was," says Allison, "evidence that a little of the real me has survived." By "the real me" Allison means his iconoclastic, vengeful side—which is a big reason why he survives. He holds a set of grudges that keep him going as much as his religion does. "The real me" is why Allison shies away from being compared with the righteous Job. He says, "Job was an entirely different kind of man."

There is no record of Job hating another man so much that he feared his own soul would wind up in hell. Allison long harbored such a hatred for fellow driver Darrell Waltrip.

Job never begrudged a monarch his throne, but Allison still leaks resentment of Richard Petty's 200 career wins and his status as the king of stock car racing.

Job did not tell prophets to kiss his ass, but that's literally what Allison told Junior Johnson, the car owner famous for his innovations, in 1972 (otherwise Allison, not Petty, might be known as NASCAR's king), and it's figuratively what he told owner Roger Penske in '76 (otherwise Allison might have been so successful in Indy Cars that he would be as celebrated for his versatility as A.J. Foyt and Mario Andretti).

And Job never beat up a peer with his fists. That's what Allison did to Cale Yarborough in 1979 in the most notorious ending ever to a Daytona 500.

These incidents may all be in Bobby's past, but emotionally they are in his present. His peeves and grudges abide as blessed distractions from his sorrow.

When Johnson sold his racing team and retired at the end of the 1995 season, after 139 victories with various drivers, he told his employees, "If we'd been able to keep Bobby Allison, we would have won 200 races, and Richard Petty wouldn't have."

As it turned out, "I won for 10 different teams," says Allison, only half proud that he quit so many owners. He was, says his brother Donnie, 57, a former driver, "his own worst enemy."

CASUALTIES DONNIE (LEFT, WITH BOBBY IN 1966) WAS SEVERELY INJURED IN A 1981 WRECK AT CHARLOTTE.

> Job did not tell the Prophets to kiss his ass, but that's literally what Allison told legendary car owner Junior Johnson in 1972.

YOUNG AND HUNGRY A LEAN, 28-YEAR-OLD ALLISON PONDERED HIS POWER IN 1966, THE YEAR HE GOT HIS FIRST CUP VICTORY.

The alltime NASCAR wins list reads: Petty, 200; David Pearson, 105; Waltrip and Bobby Allison, 84 each. "Eight-five," says Allison. "I've really got 85." Allison won a race at Winston-Salem, N.C., in 1971 in a now defunct class of car, the Grand American, that was sometimes used to fill out Winston Cup fields at backwater tracks. Petty finished second that night, but in a Winston Cup–class car. Because NASCAR officials deemed Allison's nimble little Grand American Mustang to have had an advantage over the heavier Winston Cup cars on the tiny quarter-mile oval, they later took the official victory away from him and awarded it to no one. Allison, however, believes Petty got the win, and if NASCAR were to restore it to Allison, Petty's total victories would fall short of the magical 200.

"Now who in the world would take one of the king's 200 wins away from him?" asks Allison with delicious irony in his voice. "Who in the world would do something that vile?"

Twenty-five years have passed since Petty called a truce in their war on the track. From 1967 to 1972 they had wrecked each other repeatedly, intentionally, in races across America. "Now," says Petty, "at least we can joke about it."

Sort of. Just last fall Petty was driving his pickup on Interstate 85 near Charlotte when he couldn't get past a car in the left lane. Petty tailgated, trying to get the car to move over. The other driver jammed on his brakes for spite. Petty, never one to shy away from a confrontation, bumped the offender. Petty received a traffic citation that was widely reported. At the next NASCAR race, Allison, limping past Petty in the garage, couldn't help himself. "Hey, Richard," he said. "That guy on I-85 must have looked like me."

"Nah," Petty said. "He was just acting like you."

"For career wins," says Allison, turning his guns toward Waltrip, "I am tied with a man who will probably break the tie. But if Darrell would only give back all the wins he got illegally, then he would be tied with Joe Frasson for career wins." (Frasson was a colorful but winless driver of the '70s.)

Illegally? How were Waltrip's wins illegal? "Big fuel tanks, wrong-size engines, wrong tires, you name it," says Allison. "He just got away with murder, race after race."

Waltrip laughs that off as absurd. "Bobby's a lot smarter than me," he says. "Just ask him. So if I thought of that many ways to win races illegally, how many do you think he thought of? For every race I won illegally, he won one more. Seriously, though, do you think NASCAR would let that happen, race after race?

"One of Bobby's downfalls was that he was paranoid. No matter how well he was doing, he thought everybody was against him. Particularly NASCAR—the officials."

Says Donnie Allison, "I honestly believe Bobby felt that nobody could beat him legally. I never heard him say, 'I got beat.' He always thought he was outcheated, or whatever. It became an obsession with him. And it's a sore spot with him today. Right now."

Waltrip suspects that Allison's grievances are based on races in the early '80s, when Waltrip collected most of his victories and all three of his Winston Cup championships. "I was driving for the one man Bobby hates more than he hates me: Junior Johnson," Waltrip says. All Waltrip knows for sure is that with the last words he heard Allison utter as a NASCAR driver, "he called me an a------." And Waltrip thinks Allison was gunning for him on that fateful afternoon in 1988 at Pocono. He believes Allison was still angry over their wreck in Riverside, Calif., the previous Sunday. (Each man still blames the other for the Riverside crash.)

Allison smiles about the only moment he remembers from that Pocono weekend. "Sunday morning," he says. "Drivers' meeting. They asked if there were any questions. I raised my hand. I said, 'What are you supposed to do if some a------ spins you out?' [Driver] Michael Waltrip spoke up, 'I'm not the a------. I'm just his brother.' "

"Before the race started," Darrell Waltrip says, "some of the guys who worked on Bobby's crew came up to me. They said, 'Please watch out for Bobby. He's had a terrible week, and he's crazy. He says he's gonna wreck you, and he's gonna wreck you big.' Bobby had qualified poorly and was starting toward the back of the field. I was starting up near the front. On the parade lap, I radioed my guys and said, 'Let me know if Bobby gets anywhere near me. I gotta keep an eye on him today.'

"We took the green flag, made the first lap at speed and"— Waltrip's eyes suddenly change from fiery to misty—"there he was. Sitting there. Wrecked." Allison's car had spun sideways because of a flat tire and had been T-boned on the driver's side by the car of Jocko Maggiacomo.

Waltrip throws up his hands. "I know how Bobby feels," he says. "Doesn't matter. Bobby Allison is the only man in all of racing I can walk up to and just start crying. It breaks my heart, knowing what's trapped inside that body. A man of tremendous pride. A great competitor. A leader. An innovator. I have a great deal of

admiration for him. And a great deal of compassion. My emotions for him run the gamut."

Allison cannot remember his intentions as the Pocono race started, but he doubts he was gunning for Waltrip. "Never in my career did I allow myself to carry a problem from one track to another," he says. "If I didn't take care of the situation then and there, to have waited until the next race to retaliate . . . would have been wrong."

His most notorious instance of taking care of business on the spot was with Yarborough at Daytona in '79. Yarborough and Donnie Allison wrecked while dueling for the lead on the final lap. They got out of their cars and argued but didn't fight. "Then Bobby drove up," Donnie recalls. "It is partly true that Bobby stopped to see if I was O.K. But if you could open up Bobby's head and look inside, you'd see that what was really on his mind was the first wreck that day," a less serious one that had involved all three men.

Moments after the race ended, "I was sitting in my car, strapped in," Bobby says. "Cale came over and hit me in the face with his helmet. I saw blood dripping down on my uniform. And I thought, If I don't take care of this right now, I'll be running from Cale Yarborough the rest of my life."

"How Bobby got out of that car that fast I'll never know," says Donnie. "But I knew what was going to happen. I'd seen that look on Bobby's face before. Bobby beat the s--- out of him. Hit him about three good times right in the face. Cale tried to kick him, and Bobby grabbed his foot and turned him upside down." At that point officials broke them up.

"Cale never challenged me again," says Bobby contentedly. But Donnie and Yarborough wrecked again in the next race, at Rockingham. Controversy swirled around Donnie for the rest of the season, and he never got another competitive ride. In 1981, driving a mediocre car at Charlotte, he was broadsided and suffered a life-threatening head injury. "For all practical purposes," Donnie says, "that ended my career."

Bobby didn't stop his car at the wreck scene at Charlotte that day—indeed, he went on to win the race. "If I could have done something constructive, I'd have been there," he says. "But I didn't belong."

At Pocono in '88 Davey followed family tradition, racing on after Bobby's crash even though his father might be dying or already dead. "I had watched how he handled it with Donnie," Davey later recalled.

Davey had absorbed his father's toughness since childhood—at

BOBBY'S BOYS CLIFFORD (AT AGE 2, IN HUEYTOWN) WAS ALWAYS THE IMP; DAVEY (5) WAS MORE STANDOFFISH.

I still don't know whether I blame myself about Clifford," Bobby says. "But racing took Clifford. And racing was my... my whole life."

times from a distance. "I coached both of Bobby's boys in little league football," says Donnie. "He didn't. Oh, he might show up for a game once in a while."

When Petty's son Kyle decided to become a racer, Petty made sure his son was placed in the finest equipment Petty Enterprises could offer. When Davey Allison expressed a desire to race, as Bobby once told it, "I said, 'There's the shop. There's all the tools. Go to work.'"

"Davey's first good race car, I gave him," says Donnie. "I had told his daddy, 'Why don't you give that boy a car he can go race with?' Bobby said, 'He'll do all right.' And that was it. That boy was at a stage where he needed help. And for whatever reason, he didn't get it. Davey came and got my car on a Tuesday afternoon. He won in it that Friday night."

Up through the ranks Davey went, on his own, and by February 1988 he was the best young driver in NASCAR. As the laps waned in that year's Daytona 500, only two drivers were left dueling for the win: Davey and a wily veteran—his father. Fender to fender they went, at nearly 200 mph. Surely, some observers thought, the old man would give the kid a break and let him win. But on the last lap the old man put the kid in his mirror. It was Bobby's third and last Daytona 500 victory. "It's the happiest day of my life," Davey said upon accompanying his dad to the winner's interview. "It's better than if I had won myself. . . . He's always been my hero."

Bobby remembers nothing of that race. It is part of the monthslong blank in his memory caused by his injury later that year. "I've watched the videotape several times," he says. "It only annoyed me, because I couldn't remember." Might it have been the happiest day of his life, too? "Had to be," he says, and that searching, groping look troubles his face again. "Had to be."

In 1992 Davey got his first and only Daytona 500 victory. He dedicated it to his father.

Bobby behaved differently with Clifford. Perhaps he tried to give Clifford something he hadn't given Davey. Or perhaps Clifford simply charmed him more. "When they were little boys, Clifford could be guilty and talk himself out of a whipping," says Bobby. "Davey could be innocent and talk himself into one. I was always enterprising, willing to work for everything, and that's how Davey was. Clifford felt like, why should he work when he could trick Davey into doing the work for him?"

Bobby carries one photograph with him always. "This tells the whole story," he says, opening his wallet. He holds out a picture taken in the spring of 1992 of his sons seated together at dinner. Behind Davey's head, Clifford holds up two fingers. "There's Davey, doing what he's supposed to do, smiling for the camera," Bobby says. "And there's his little brother, giving him a set of horns and loving it, and Davey doesn't know it."

From 1989 into the summer of '92 Bobby nurtured Clifford's climb through Busch Grand National racing, NASCAR's version of Triple A. "And Clifford was stimulating me so much," Bobby says. The old man's recovery from his accident was quickening. "He was living through Clifford," Judy says.

"Working with Clifford was his therapy," says Kitty Allison. "But when Clifford died, it stymied Bobby."

"He had just turned a really fast lap in that practice session," says Bobby. "He came into the garage, and his crew made some minor adjustments. As he backed out of the garage to go back out on the track, he looked at me and grinned and said, 'We're gonna get 'em, Dad.' His last words to me were, 'We're gonna get 'em, Dad.'" Bobby's voice dwindles to a whisper. "'We're gonna get 'em, Dad.'

"He went back out. Then suddenly his crew chief threw down his radio headset and said, 'He crashed.' I said, 'Is he O.K.?' The crew chief put the headset back on and said, 'Clifford? Are you O.K.? Clifford, can you hear me? Clifford? Clifford?'

"I started walking. All the safety vehicles came tearing down the pit road the wrong way—very unusual. Out on the track I saw Bobby Labonte stop his car, get out and look into Clifford's car. Then Labonte stepped back, climbed back in his car and drove away. I kept walking. A NASCAR official came up and said, 'Bobby, they don't want you out there.' I said, 'That's my son. I'm going.' He said, 'I'll walk with you.' And I walked up to that car. . . .

"After that, Davey became really attentive to me. He would always say, 'Come on, Dad, go with me in my plane.' Or, 'Come on, Dad, let's go get a bite to eat.' I rode home with him from the '93 New Hampshire race in his Cheyenne airplane. I sat in the copilot seat. We talked about all kinds of things. Some old things. Some current things. His outlook. His ambitions. The next morning I had a [physical] therapy session and then went to my office, down the hill there from the house. I was on the phone. Another line rang. Donnie Johnson [Allison's brother-in-law and former business manager] answered it. He listened, and he looked at me and said, 'Hang up the phone.' He had never said such a thing to me before. I looked

FATHER'S DAY ON THE LAST LAP OF THE 1988 DAYTONA 500, BOBBY (12) SNATCHED THE VICTORY FROM SON DAVEY.

I f I get killed in a race car," Davey Allison once said, his brown eyes blazing with certainty, "I'm gonna die with a smile on my face."

at him. He said, 'Hang up the phone. And get that other line.' The other line said Davey's helicopter had crashed at Talladega.

"I went to the house and told Judy we had to go. We got to the hospital in Birmingham before the rescue helicopter got there with Davey. They were gathering doctors. There was one they had a lot of confidence in for head injuries. They worked on Davey for about three hours. Then they said we'd have to wait and see.

"I went and found a room by myself. I waited there for an incredibly long night." Just after dawn Davey died.

The next morning, down at his racing shop at the end of Church Avenue, Bobby buried his face in the chest of a journalist he had known for a long time, and he wept as hard as a man can weep and remain standing. "It hurts!" he sobbed. Then he screamed, "Ohhhh, it hurts!"

But only hours later, after Davey's funeral, Bobby stood in the front yard at 135 Church Avenue, smiled and told the same journalist, "My religion teaches me that I have to forgive everyone of everything. But no one can convince me that I have to forgive Darrell Waltrip."

Allison now says that over the years, through long talks with Waltrip's deeply religious wife, Stevie, he has given up many of his grievances against Darrell. "I may—I probably will—end up down there shoveling coal with the little red guy," Allison says, "but I'm gonna tell you something: I still have forgiven Darrell Waltrip only three fourths." Maybe those grudges that give Allison relief really are Godsent.

On a Tuesday morning, Kitty Allison drives home to 136 Church Avenue from early Mass. She sits down at her kitchen table and begins to work on her Avon cosmetic accounts before leaving on her sales calls. She may be the sharpest, strongest, most active—in other words, the most independent—90-year-old woman on earth. Bobby has just left for Mobile, where he will see Jeremiah Denton, a Vietnam War hero, later a U.S. senator and the author of Bobby's favorite book, *When Hell Was in Session*. Denton is recovering from cancer, and Bobby has always kept the Catholic tradition of visiting sick friends.

Kitty's home is filled with religious articles, mostly statues of the Virgin. The Mother of God gazes down from the front room wall at every visitor who enters. Beside Kitty on the sofa is a newly framed certificate proclaiming the apostolic blessing of His Holiness Pope John Paul II upon Katherine Allison on the occasion of her 90th birthday. "There is some reason," she says, her eyes welling

CAN'T GO HOME FACED WITH CRUSHING MEDICAL BILLS AFTER HIS ACCIDENT, ALLISON PUT HIS HOUSE UP FOR SALE.

Just seeing Bobby," says his mother, "don't you realize what a miracle it is? They never dreamed he would recover to be the man he is."

NOT FADE AWAY DESPITE HIS LOSSES AND HIS INJURIES, AT AGE 66 BOBBY ALLISON IS ON HIS FEET AND LOOKING AHEAD.

with tears, "some reason all of this has happened. We don't know what it is. But there's some reason. Someday we hope to find out." Her face grows staunch, and her tears disappear. She says, "Don't you realize what a miracle it is?"

Beg your pardon?

"Just seeing Bobby. Don't you realize what a miracle it is? They never dreamed he would recover to be the man he is. Not one of the doctors dreamed." Her eyes mist, and her voice cracks. "But this latest thing, with his marriage, he's going to have to work out for himself." She prays for a reconciliation between Bobby and Judy.

Bonnie often stops by to see her father and grandmother, though Bobby is usually out traveling in his beloved Aerostar. Each time she visits, she cannot help gazing across the street. "That big old empty house sitting over there just eats at me, every day," Bonnie says. "My husband and I would move in—in a heartbeat—but we can't afford to buy it. Dad gave it to Mom, and she can't seem to sell it for what she wants. Just seeing it sitting there, rotting to pieces, is sad." Bonnie's voice breaks. "Just sad."

But for Judy, seeing the house so forlorn is no more difficult to bear than living in what, for fans, had become a shrine. "People wanted to come by there," she says. "They wanted to see where Bobby lived, where Davey had lived, where Clifford had lived. They liked to ring the doorbell. They had gone to the cemetery and left pennies or roses or some memorabilia. And then they liked to tell you things. A lot of times it was good things, and that was great. But they also liked to cry on your shoulder. I don't want them to feel bad about it—they were just trying to express their sympathy—but people just don't realize, you know?

"The memories of the children in the house are wonderful. But when you throw in financial problems, and you throw in all these people coming by, and—where was Bobby? Bobby was either at the shop or out flying. So he didn't have to contend with all of this as much as I did. So things just kind of went in a different direction, and the next thing I knew, this is where we're at."

"I have learned to launder my underwear," says Bobby. "I have learned to cook spaghetti. And I will make it."

Just how much can one man bear?

"I am afraid," he says, "to ask that question." □

"he NFL has the Super Bowl, baseball has the World Series, and now NASCAR has this season-ending race in the Chase. I've never driven so hard in my life."

SEAT OF POWER AFTER COPPING THE CUP AT HOMESTEAD, KURT BUSCH SAVORED THE SPOILS OF VICTORY.

PHOTOGRAPH BY BILL FRAKES